"John Allen has been a prophetic voice on behalf of Christians suffering persecution around the world. This book reminds us, who can practice our religion without fear, that some of our brothers and sisters live in constant peril."

—Thomas Reese, SJ
Columnist, *National Catholic Reporter*

"As God always brings good out of evil, He has raised up heroes to fight for the dignity and rights of the persecuted. One such hero was the Servant of God Shahbaz Bhatti of Pakistan. In this book, John Allen beautifully and lovingly tells the story of his life—and martyrdom."

—Robert P. George
McCormick Professor of Jurisprudence
Princeton University

"The story of Shahbaz Bhatti, slain for his outspoken criticism of Pakistan's blasphemy laws, is an important and disturbing lesson on anti-Christian persecution. It's a must-read for Catholics who care about religious freedom. Allen does not skip over the criticism Bhatti faced, even among some Christians, for his 'pugnacious' activism and his use of partisan politics in the advancement of religious rights. Yet he makes a strong case for considering Bhatti a modern martyr and a patron of religious freedom."

—John Thavis, author of *The Vatican Diaries*

People of God

Remarkable Lives, Heroes of Faith

People of God is a series of inspiring biographies for the general reader. Each volume offers a compelling and honest narrative of the life of an important twentieth- or twenty-first-century Catholic. Some living and some now deceased, each of these women and men has known challenges and weaknesses familiar to most of us but responded to them in ways that call us to our own forms of heroism. Each offers a credible and concrete witness of faith, hope, and love to people of our own day.

John XXIII	Massimo Faggioli
Oscar Romero	Kevin Clarke
Thomas Merton	Michael W. Higgins
Francis	Michael Collins
Flannery O'Connor	Angela O'Donnell
Martin Sheen	Rose Pacatte
Jean Vanier	Michael W. Higgins
Dorothy Day	Patrick Jordan
Luis Antonio Tagle	Cindy Wooden
Georges and Pauline Vanier	Mary Francis Coady
Joseph Bernardin	Steven P. Millies
Corita Kent	Rose Pacatte
Daniel Rudd	Gary B. Agee
Helen Prejean	Joyce Duriga
Paul VI	Michael Collins
Thea Bowman	Maurice J. Nutt
Shahbaz Bhatti	John L. Allen Jr.
Rutilio Grande	Rhina Guidos

More titles to follow . . .

Shahbaz Bhatti

*Martyr of
the Suffering Church*

John L. Allen Jr.

LITURGICAL PRESS
Collegeville, Minnesota

www.litpress.org

Cover design by Red+Company. Cover illustration by Philip Bannister.

© 2017 by Order of Saint Benedict, Collegeville, Minnesota. All rights reserved. No part of this book may be reproduced in any form, by print, microfilm, microfiche, mechanical recording, photocopying, translation, or by any other means, known or yet unknown, for any purpose except brief quotations in reviews, without the previous written permission of Liturgical Press, Saint John's Abbey, PO Box 7500, Collegeville, Minnesota 56321-7500. Printed in the United States of America.

Library of Congress Control Number: 2017940903

ISBN 978-0-8146-4623-6   978-0-8146-4648-9 (ebook)

Contents

Introduction 1

Chapter One
Roots 13

Chapter Two
Christians in Pakistan 25

Chapter Three
All-Pakistan Minorities Alliance 40

Chapter Four
Minister for Minorities Affairs 58

Chapter Five
Death Comes for the Minister 78

Chapter Six
Sainthood 98

Conclusion 116

Index 127

Introduction

Every human life is remarkable in its own way, often full of hidden drama and quiet tumult. Those who glimpse and discern larger truths at even the most micro level are part of what the poet William Blake meant in extolling the fine art of seeing "a world in a grain of sand, and heaven in a wild flower."

What the wider world comes to know and appreciate about any individual life is often a combination of how compelling the person's story is in itself and how it intersects with the larger movements and tensions of the time. Nelson Mandela's biography, for instance, would be riveting under any set of circumstances, but through both his reflection and driving a larger movement for the elimination of apartheid, his story took on global significance and made Mandela the leading example in his era of what some observers these days are calling "secular saints."

In similar fashion, a Polish bishop named Karol Wojtyla would probably have inspired a few biographies under any set of circumstances—a fairly daring philosopher and playwright with an utterly novel approach to youth ministry rooted in his experience as a college chaplain. But by becoming Pope John Paul II and playing a lead role in the collapse of European Communism, he became a global sensation and has been recognized as a saint by the church he led.

A Pakistani human rights activist, politician, and devoted Roman Catholic named Shahbaz Bhatti is a perfect illustration of this formula for significance.

On its own, his life was the stuff of a Hollywood movie. He was born in the globally tumultuous year of 1968 in a village in the Punjab region of Pakistan to a father who was a former army officer and teacher and a stay-at-home mother. He was always deeply religious. As a young man he was an altar boy, traveling with his parish priest to serve Masses in neighboring villages, and later he founded a youth Bible study group in his parish.

There are roughly 2.5 million Christians in Pakistan, representing fewer than 2 percent of the overwhelmingly Muslim nation population. It was in college that Bhatti first felt the sting of persecution because of his minority status.

"There were many Christian students who experienced discrimination . . . they were beaten and tortured because the Islamic extremists didn't want them to study," he recalled in a 2005 interview.

Later Bhatti founded the All-Pakistan Minorities Alliance, the country's premier organization fighting for the emancipation of religious and ethnic minority groups. Beyond political advocacy, the group also engaged in direct service to the vulnerable, for example, playing a heroic role in relief efforts after a massive 2005 earthquake in Kashmir that left an estimated 88,000 people dead.

Bhatti was so successful as an activist and human rights champion he was named Federal Minister for Minorities Affairs in 2008, making him the lone Christian in Pakistan's cabinet, and he used that perch to press for further reform, especially abolition of the country's notorious blasphemy laws. He publicly called for the release and exoneration of Asia Bibi, an illiterate Catholic mother of five from the Punjab, who was sentenced to death under the blasphemy laws, following a dispute with some Muslim women in her village over access to drinking water.

By 2011 it seemed clear that Bhatti was swimming against the tide in a Pakistan whose Islamic community had undergone the same pressures of radicalization as other Muslim nations. In January of that year, the Muslim governor of Bhatti's home region of Punjab, Salmaan Taseer, was shot to death by radicals for his own opposition to the blasphemy laws. Three months later they came for Bhatti, gunning him down in a residential neighborhood of Islamabad, the national capital, shortly after he had left his mother's home. Ironically, his older sister Jacqueline said he had come to express concern for his mother's safety, and his last words before leaving were "take care of yourself."

Bhatti's car was riddled with bullets; investigators later pegged the number of separate shots at twenty-seven. Authorities initially tried to blame his death on a family dispute or perhaps on financial irregularities in his personal life or the government ministry he led. Quickly, however, the terrorist group Tehrik-i-Taliban took responsibility for the murder, boasting about having slain a "known blasphemer."

On March 31, 2011, the Catholic bishops of Pakistan wrote to then-Pope Benedict XVI to say they had unanimously approved a petition that Bhatti be enrolled "in the martyrology of the universal church," meaning declared a saint. After the church's customary five-year waiting period for the launch of a sainthood cause expired in 2016, a procedure for his eventual beatification and canonization has been formally opened by the Diocese of Islamabad-Rawalpindi. Although politics may slow things down, Bhatti is now known as a "Servant of God" and may one day be explicitly recognized as a Catholic saint.

Under any set of circumstances, such a life and death would be compelling. Bhatti was a driven believer who repeatedly put his life on the line to serve others and whose advocacy for his own community broadened into a vigorous and heartfelt defense of religious freedom for all. By itself his story would be enough to stir the imagination, and it's done just that. A pop band in the United Kingdom named Ooberfuse released a single called "Blood Cries Out" in honor of Bhatti on the first anniversary of his death in 2012. He also has been the subject of countless posthumous awards, biographies, celebrations, and monuments, including several from Muslims, Hindus, Sikhs, and other minority groups who saw Bhatti as a friend and champion.

Yet that's not the complete picture, because what elevates Bhatti's life to the level of truly global significance is the way it so neatly captures the most dramatic human rights situation, bar none, of the early twenty-first century—a global pandemic of anti-Christian violence and persecution, making Bhatti the perfect patron saint for Christianity's sadly abundant harvest of new martyrs.

The Global War on Christians

Since the rest of this book will be devoted to Bhatti's story, this section explains why his story represents the broader Christian story of today's era.

Though precise counts of victims are notoriously difficult to determine, it's widely acknowledged in terms of raw numbers that Christians today are by far the world's most persecuted religious body, a point current German chancellor Angela Merkel stated in November 2012 and former British prime minister David Cameron confirmed in April 2014.

In part that's because Christianity is the world's largest religious body with 2.3 billion adherents, meaning that statistically speaking Christians are more exposed to harm. By way of comparison, there are roughly 1.7 billion Muslims. Further, the zones of Christianity's greatest growth today, including sub-Saharan Africa and parts of Asia, are often regions where religious freedom is more honored in the breach than the observance. Another factor is that due to the psychological and political tendency in many quarters to identify Christianity with the West, in various global hot spots, radical groups with axes to grind against Western economic or military policies often take out those frustrations on local Christian communities, despite the irony that those communities often have far deeper roots in the area than the radicals themselves do.

Whatever the explanation, the numbers are harrowing.

- According to the Pew Research Center on Religion and Public Life (a widely respected secular think tank in Washington, DC, not sponsored by any church or confessional organization), between 2006 and 2010 Christians had been harassed either *de jure* or *de facto* in 139 nations, more than two-thirds of all the countries on earth, and had the highest total for any religious group. The center found the total alone in 2016 was 108 nations out of 198 surveyed, up from 102 in 2013.

- The National Consortium for the Study of Terrorism and Responses to Terrorism (known by the acronym START) was established in 2005 by the US Department of Homeland Security and is based at the University of Maryland. In 2003 the group found that Christians were explicitly attacked by terrorists in Africa, Asia, and the Middle East eleven times, while in 2010

Christians faced forty-five such assaults. As the START analysis points out, that represents a stunning growth rate of 309 percent in just seven years.

- The evangelical advocacy and relief organization Open Doors has been providing aid to persecuted Christians since it was founded in 1955 by a Dutch Protestant named Andrew van der Bijl, better known as "Brother Andrew," who began by smuggling Bibles into the Soviet sphere. In its 2016 annual report, the group estimated that 215 million Christians around the world face the threat of legal discrimination, physical assault, arrest, torture, and even death on a daily basis.

- In January 2013 Fr. John E. Kozar, a longtime expert on the Middle East and the Secretary of the Catholic Near East Welfare Association, estimated that there were 25 million Christians in the Middle East alone "exposed to situations of poverty, and victims of war and persecution."

- The high-end estimate for the number of Christians killed every year for reasons linked to their faith comes from the Center for the Study of Global Christianity, which puts the total at roughly 100,000. Others, including Thomas Schirrmacher, a spokesman for the World Council of Churches, believe the total is much lower, perhaps 7,000 to 8,000. That works out to a range between one new Christian martyr every five minutes and one every hour.

As disturbing as those numbers are, they only really come alive when one attaches names, voices, and faces to them, as a reminder that underneath every broad trend is the reality of an individual life. The following are simply three almost randomly chosen examples.

Sr. Meena Lalita Barwa is a Catholic nun who was serving in Kandhamal, India, in the summer of 2008 when she and a local priest, Fr. Thomas Chellen, were dragged into the streets by frenzied Hindu radicals shouting, "Kill Christians!" They attempted to force Chellen to rape Barwa, and when he refused they beat him severely. They stopped only because they thought he was dead, but miraculously he survived.

Barwa, the niece of Archbishop John Barwa of Cuttack-Bhubaneswar, was raped by at least one man—she can't remember the number as she lost consciousness during the attack—and later was paraded partially naked through the streets of the village while the mob continued to howl.

Today Barwa, who comes from India's long-marginalized indigenous tribal peoples, is working on a law degree to fight for justice for other victims, and she takes comfort in a spiritual explanation of her ordeal. "Because Jesus Christ wasn't a woman, there were certain kinds of suffering he couldn't experience in his own body in order to save the world," she says. "I like to think I helped to complete his sacrifice."

Chioma Dike is a Nigerian Catholic and a mother of five who lost her husband and three children in a Boko Haram bomb blast at St. Theresa's Church in Madalla, about an hour outside the capital city of Abuja, on Christmas Day 2011.

Remarkably, she says she has no hatred for those who tore her family apart. "I'm not angry," she said in an August 2015 interview. "I pray for God to forgive them, because they don't know what they are doing."

Bishop Misael Vacca Ramirez of the diocese of Duitama-Sogamoso, Colombia, was kidnapped in 2004 and held for three days by one of his country's left-wing guerrilla movements.

A bloody civil war in Colombia has dragged on for almost sixty years, leaving an estimated 220,000 dead and more than 90,000 "disappeared." Vacca knew he could be killed, too, joining two other bishops and eighty-five Colombian priests who have died as a result of the violence.

Speaking at his modest family home in Bogotá in the summer of 2015, Vacca began to tell his story and then abruptly stopped, seized by tears. He explained that he was thinking of all those people who died instead of making it out alive, often forgotten and alone. "So many victims," he said. "So much pain."

For far too long such chapters in anti-Christian violence were hidden by a vast wall of silence. As French intellectual Régis Debray, a veteran leftist who fought alongside Che Guevara, pointed out, anti-Christian persecution falls into the ideological "blind spot" of the West, with the victims being too religious to interest the left and too foreign and third-world to excite the right.

After the rise of ISIS and the explicit recognition of anti-Christian "genocide" in the Middle East by most major world powers, including the United States State Department, such denial is more difficult to sustain, but it remains the case that the vast scale of Christian martyrdom in our time, and its truly global character, still has not excited anything like the public outrage and political mobilization the situation merits.

For example, as of early 2017 the vast majority of Christian victims of ISIS were receiving no assistance from public agencies such as the UN and USAID because they refuse to enter the massive refugee and IDP camps funded by those same bodies out of fear of further exposure to Islamic radicals, so victims are entirely dependent on the church. Yet public agencies decline to turn over a portion of their budget for humanitarian relief to the institutional church to ensure it reaches needy Christians, largely over hang-ups about church-state separation. The net result is that the US government has officially recognized Christians in Iraq and Syria as the victims of genocide yet is investing essentially zero in meaningful relief efforts to help them stay alive.

Whenever discussing this global war on Christians, two caveats always have to be read into the record to avoid misunderstanding.

First, it's not as if Christian suffering is any more dramatic or noble than the suffering of anyone else. Christians are hardly the only group facing violent persecution today, and if a defense of religious freedom is to mean anything, it must be applied across the board for everyone. It must be a universal cause rather than one driven exclusively by narrow confessional self-interest.

In fact there's nothing confessional about the cause of defending vulnerable Christians at all. Just as one did not have to be Jewish in the 1960s and 1970s to be concerned about dissident Jews in the Soviet Union or black in the 1980s to be outraged by the apartheid system in South Africa, one hardly needs to be Christian today to recognize this as the transcendent human rights cause of the day.

Second, concern for anti-Christian persecution does not imply any position whatsoever in what Westerners typically call the "culture wars" and should not be swept up into the left vs. right dynamic of Western politics. To say that an illiterate Dalit woman, meaning a member of the "underclass" under the ancient caste system, should not be hacked to death simply because of her religious beliefs, is worlds apart from American debates over the contraception mandates imposed by the Affordable Care Act as part of healthcare reform or the right of public officials, such as former

Kentucky County Clerk Kim Davis, to exercise conscientious objection from gay marriage laws. Whether one sees a slippery slope beginning with the latter and leading to the former or not, they remain distinct.

Both liberals and conservatives in Western affairs need to recognize anti-Christian persecution for what it truly is—a human rights issue, not a political one, and its victims should not be doubly victimized by either being ignored or artificially lionized to score rhetorical points in debates to which they're completely extraneous.

Shahbaz Bhatti as Patron Saint

The context of the global war on Christians relates to the individual saga of Shahbaz Bhatti because it establishes three basic points.

- Anti-Christian persecution is the most compelling Christian drama of our time, one in which any Christian anywhere ought to feel a stake.

- It's also the most underreported and underappreciated human rights scourge of our time, a transcendent social cause waiting to catch fire in the hearts and minds of all people of goodwill, regardless of their religious beliefs.

- While statistics and overviews provide necessary support for that cause, the individual stories of the new martyrs will best capture the imagination.

That is the true power of Bhatti's life—he puts a riveting and deeply attractive face on this vast company of martyrdom, making him potentially the ideal patron saint for the cause.

There can be no doubt of Bhatti's deep Catholic piety. In a video recorded shortly before his death, he said, "I know Jesus Christ who sacrificed his life for others. I understand well the meaning of the cross. I am ready to give my life for my people." After he was assassinated, his brother Paul recounted cleaning out Shahbaz's spartan apartment, where the only three items on a small bedside table were the Bible, a rosary, and a picture of the Virgin Mary.

In death as in life, Bhatti stood with followers of other religions committed to defending human rights and the rule of law. In the Pakistani mind, his memory is inevitably linked to that of Taseer, a Muslim, making both of them "secular saints" among moderates and believers in democracy, well ahead of any formal declaration by a religious body. Bhatti's story thus encapsulates the truth that striving to defend Christians from persecution does not require hostility to any other religious group; instead, it's an enterprise best carried out in collaboration with those groups.

Bhatti defended the rights of Hindus, Sikhs, and others with equal vigor, not to mention Muslims. Paul Bhatti said that point was brought home for him at his brother's funeral: "I saw this sea of people, gripped by uncontrollable emotion," he said. "My brother was a symbol not just for Christians but for other minorities, and even for very many Muslims."

None of this is to say that Bhatti's legacy is without question marks. He moved in the complex, often fallen world of politics, and he had his critics. Some saw him as a showboat fundamentally interested in his own celebrity, while some of his fellow Christians thought he had been co-opted by the prestige of a cabinet post toward the end and was no longer sufficiently vigorous in criticizing the government he served. All of that, and much more, will no doubt be examined in painstaking detail in the church's official sainthood process, before reaching a definitive judgment about whether he truly lived a life of "heroic virtue."

What can be said with certainty is that few contemporary biographies better illustrate the broader realities of the situation facing Christians all around the world in the early twenty-first century than that of Shahbaz Bhatti, which makes his story all the more worth telling.

CHAPTER ONE

Roots

Though it's an overused phrase, one could almost say that Shahbaz Bhatti was "born for some sort of Catholic greatness." He entered the world on September 9, 1968, in the village of Khushpur in Pakistan's Punjab region, a settlement founded in 1899 by Capuchin priests, which has been described by Linda Walbridge in her 2012 book *The Christians of Pakistan* as "more like a missionary colony than a real village."

Tradition says the founder of the village was a Capuchin named Fr. Felix, which explains the name. *Felix* is the Latin word for "happy," and in the local Urdu language, *Khushpur* means "the land of happy," or in this case "the land of Father Felix." To this day, every year in October there's a procession through the streets of Khushpur that draws Catholics from all over the country, featuring live biblical scenes enacted on street corners. Among Pakistani Catholics, the village is sometimes known as "little Italy" because of its overtly Catholic ethos. Khushpur is one of fifty-three such villages founded throughout Pakistan by religious congregations, mostly before the partition from India in 1947. It also boasts the lone National Catechist Training Centre in Pakistan, with catechists from all across the country coming to the village to study.

Walbridge describes walking through the Khushpur cemetery and coming across the headstone of an American woman named Regina Elsa Wilam, who was born in 1954 and died in 1995. According to one of the nuns at the convent school in the village, Wilam had been excited by stories narrated by Capuchins over the years about their mission work in Pakistan, and in her will asked that her remains be transferred to Khushpur and buried there as a sort of eternal statement of solidarity with the local Catholic community.

The church's imprint on Khushpur is also reflected in the long list of Catholic notables the village has produced over the years, including the late Bishop Rufin Anthony who led the Islamabad-Rawalpindi Diocese; noted writer and scholar Allama Paul Ernest; and the politician Simon Jacob Gill, a former member of the National Assembly.

Perhaps most harrowingly similar to Bhatti's own story is that of another native son of Khushpur, Bishop John Joseph, whose life and death was always a source of inspiration for Bhatti. Born in Khushpur in 1932, Joseph was ordained in 1960, and during Vatican II he studied for his theology doctorate at St. Thomas University in Rome. He became an auxiliary bishop of Faisalabad in 1981 and took over as diocesan bishop in 1984.

Joseph became an outspoken critic of Muslim mistreatment of Christians, leading two nationwide protests against the country's blasphemy laws and at one point launching a hunger strike. He anguished over the situation to such an extent that on May 6, 1998, after a Christian man named Ayub Masih had been executed over trumped-up blasphemy charges for alleged insults to Islam, Joseph shot himself to death in a courthouse compound in protest—the very spot where Masih had been killed.

Almost twenty years later, some Pakistani Christians remain convinced that Joseph's death wasn't a suicide, suspecting a cover-up for an assassination, although the country's bishops at one point stated that he died by his own hand.

Once upon a time, the Catholic ethos in villages such as Khsushpur and nearby Francisabad was so pervasive that priests not only presided at weddings, they essentially brokered the marriages. Father John Rooney, in his book on the roots of Pakistani Christianity, *Into Deserts*, described the scene: "When the first young men in Maryabad . . . needed to be married, they asked the priest to find suitable young women. A bunch of marriageable girls was then sent from an orphanage. . . . The young folks met and made their choices. The girls then went to the convent to await their wedding day."

Local lore in these Catholic villages tells what often happened. The boys would line up on one side of the parish meeting hall and the girls on the other, and the priest would help pair them with one another. Parish records in the villages often show several weddings being celebrated on the same day, the fruit of these arranged meet-and-match sessions organized by the church.

Although church practices had begun to loosen up by 1968 as part of the post–Vatican II period in Catholic life, Bhatti was brought up in a pervasively Catholic environment. His father, Jacob, a former army officer and teacher, took early retirement in order to devote himself virtually full time to service as the president of his parish council, and his mother, a homemaker, took pains to ensure that Bhatti and his five brothers and a sister were brought up in the faith—as if the fact that three of the children were named

Paul, Peter, and Clement wasn't enough of a clue. Jacob Bhatti died of a heart attack shortly before Shahbaz was killed, reportedly not long after receiving a menacing phone call from the Pakistani Taliban. Shahbaz's mother and siblings were still alive at the time of his death when he was forty-two.

"I was a regular churchgoer and was deeply inspired by Christ's teachings, sacrifice and crucifixion," Bhatti told Monsignor Dino Pistolato of Venice, Italy, in a 2005 interview when Pistolato was part of a delegation from the Patriarchate of Venice that traveled to Pakistan to help in earthquake relief efforts.

Friends say Bhatti was committed to individual daily prayer, and that Psalm 23, "The Lord is my shepherd," was a favorite. His attachment to the psalm highlights an important dimension of inculturation of the church in Pakistan, especially among those from the Punjabi community. The psalms were translated at an early stage into Punjabi, and they are often sung in the form of lively folk songs, making them an important part of popular Catholic religiosity.

While still in his early teens, Bhatti also established a youth group at his parish, devoted especially to Bible study. He said it was a means of "sharing in some tangible and meaningful way the warmth of Christ's love." The group would come together to read the Bible and to pray, and non-Catholic Christian students were invited to join them. In what would become a hallmark of Bhatti's approach, those spiritual aims were combined with direct humanitarian service, in this case trying to raise donations to help poor students in the group continue their studies.

Clan membership is all important in rural Pakistan, and the Bhatti clan is one of roughly five that have long held leadership positions in Khsushpur, in part because its members are among the landowning *zamindar* elite, as opposed to the landless *kammi* underclass. The Bhattis owned four acres of land, which are now farmed by Shahbaz's brother Sikander. As a result it was natural for his father to serve as the de facto head of the local Catholic community, and equally natural for the young Bhatti also feel destined to lead.

By nature an activist, Bhatti's budding religious sense was never an abstraction but quickly translated itself into concrete action. He became an altar boy in his local parish, volunteering to serve an early daily morning Mass. Quickly his responsibilities expanded, as local priests began taking him along when they went to visit and say Mass in other rural villages. Bhatti would recall that the experience of assisting the priests on those trips gave him an early crash course in the realities of Christian life in Pakistan, including the grinding poverty and chronic mistreatment many Christians endured. Later Bhatti said:

> The appalling state of Christians in Pakistan made my heart weep. . . . I remember, it was on Good Friday just before Easter when I was 13 years old, I heard a sermon on how Jesus sacrificed, gave us redemption and salvation in this world. This was a moment when I thought to reflect on Jesus' love for us, but also to respond to his love by demonstrating love for our fellow men and women, which led me to manifest Christ's love and sacrifice in my life by serving Christians, especially the poor, persecuted and victimized in this Islamic country.

Given that the Bhattis were a relatively high-status, middle-class family, the indignities faced by many of his fellow Catholics was something of a revelation for Bhatti. Many Pakistani Catholics are descendants of converts from the *Chuhra* caste of sweepers who converted to Christianity in the nineteenth century when the Punjab was under British rule. Sweepers were usually considered to be on the lowest level of South Asian society, since they dealt with filth and pollution on a daily basis. Conversion, it was hoped, would bring change in this social status, though for many Pakistani Christians the low social standing endures.

Though some Pakistani Catholics have had important positions and have been influential in national life, the vast majority of Catholics are poor, manual laborers who work on farms, operate looms for carpet making, or operate brick kilns. Kiln workers live as virtual slaves since they are bonded to repay virtually unpayable debts. Weavers are often no better off, with many working in sweatshop conditions from ages as young as four. Illiteracy is also quite high among indigenous Pakistani Christians, both Catholic and Protestant.

The Birth of an Activist

In other circumstances, watching the flowering of a devout and talented young Catholic man from a large Catholic family naturally would have beckoned thoughts of a future as a Catholic priest, perhaps one day a bishop or even a cardinal. From the beginning, however, it seemed clear that Bhatti's vocation probably lay somewhere else, in the contentious arena of political activism.

Bhatti's older brother Paul, a medical doctor who studied in Padova in Italy and Leuven in Belgium and then worked in Italy, would later return to Pakistan to take up his brother's legacy. He recalls that in 1982, when Shahbaz was just fourteen, he led a protest against a proposal to require Christians in Pakistan to carry special identity cards, which the Christians read as a way of helping authorities and radicals to identify them and discriminate against them. The determined, teenaged Bhatti traveled to Islamabad to lead a hunger strike on the steps of the parliament building, and the proposal was eventually withdrawn.

"I saw then how a strong faith could change things that seemed difficult, if not impossible, to change," Paul Bhatti said in a 2012 interview in Rome, where he was attending a Catholic Action conference to be honored for continuing his brother's work.

When Bhatti went away to college, his activist streak continued to flourish. He established an organization for Christian students to unite them and defend their rights, saying of that chapter in his life, "They felt alone, but we stood beside them."

"At that time, I was beaten by the Islamists," Bhatti said in 2005. "They asked me not to create a Christian organization, otherwise I would be killed. But I said, 'No, I am not disturbing you, I am only forming this association for my Christian brothers and sisters.' They replied, 'No, we cannot allow you.' After that day, they tortured me many times and threatened to kill me if I continued."

The organization Bhatti founded in 1985 while studying for a master's degree in political science and public administration at the University of the Punjab, Lahore, was called the Christian Liberation Front. Despite its ominous-sounding name, it was devoted to finding nonviolent means to carry forward the struggle for Christian emancipation. Fundamentally, the group's agenda, beyond simple mutual self-support, was to restore the rights of Pakistan's religious minorities and to promote tolerance.

Bhatti created the Christian Liberation Front in collaboration with Bishop Rufin Anthony, who at the time was a seminary professor. The two met when Bhatti was still attending school in Khushpur, and they kept in touch over the years. Anthony would later say of Bhatti, "He was always ready to work for the nation," calling him "steadfast" and "such an inspiration to all who profess the Christian faith." Their partnership was indicative of another characteristic trait of Bhatti's career—while he would call his own shots and do things his own way, he always preferred to move in concert with the official leadership of the church rather than being at odds with them.

The push for Christian rights, needless to say, wasn't exactly welcomed by everyone in Lahore, especially at a time when Islamic radical movements in the country were being encouraged and promoted under President Muhammad Zia-ul-Haq, who ruled from 1977 until 1988. The group experienced violent blowback from the very beginning.

Bhatti said, "Once, after I got beaten up, I complained to a professor, who replied, 'I cannot do anything.' Again we held a meeting of Christian students at college, and again I was beaten. There was a college notice board, where every organization posted its notices. So on the next day, I posted one which read: 'I can die for my Jesus, but I cannot stop uniting my Christian brothers and sisters, especially the students.'"

In another feature of Bhatti's career that would later become the stuff of legend, that act of defiance led a swell of students to join his crusade, which he described as defending "oppressed Christians from the shackles of persecution, discrimination and prejudice that prevail in the majority of Muslim society." The group provided free tuition and books to poor Christian students and promoted the idea of getting a college education in the country's Christian communities, where such ideas had long been regarded as fanciful and unattainable.

During his university studies, Bhatti became close friends with a fellow Christian named Khalil Tahir Sindhu, who today serves as Punjab's minister for human rights. The two lived together as roommates for almost seven years in a hostel in Faisalabad, named for Pope John Paul II. Both were budding politicos in the making, even running against one another twice for a student government position known as prefect. Sindhu laughingly recalls that Bhatti prevailed once and he won once, leaving them even. However, they shared the same basic political outlook: "Politics was our main area of interest, and minority rights was our pet topic," Sindhu recalled in a 2015 interview. "We would often discuss the blasphemy law, which particularly endangers minorities."

Father Tomás King, a Columban missionary in Pakistan, has written that it was also during Bhatti's university years, in his early twenties, when he decided not to marry in order to devote himself unreservedly to the struggle for minority rights and peace and justice. As King notes, in a society that puts such a premium on family, "it was a very countercultural choice to make," and probably suggests that although Bhatti had discerned the priesthood was not the right path for his life, there was nevertheless a strong priestly dimension to his own sense of vocation.

Part of the Bhatti legend dates to this university period in his life, when a strong flood in Punjab inundated several local villages. Bhatti and his friends collected donations from the university community and others in Lahore, and then set off to try to be of help. When they arrived, they saw one house in particular that had been cut off by rising floodwaters, leaving the occupants trapped. Although his friends tried to dissuade him, they would later report that Bhatti was determined to help and persuaded four friends to join. As soon as they set out, Bhatti had water up to his neck and struggled not to get stuck in the muck. The group started shivering against the cold and feared for their lives. Somehow they made it to the house and found a couple and their two small children. Placing the children on their shoulders and propping up the couple, they made it back to land safely.

"During this experience, I felt the fear of danger," Bhatti said years later. "But the spiritual strength, the blessing and the spiritual potential keep us going and defeat the fear of death. I defeated the fear of danger with the power of the Holy Spirit, with God's blessing." He would always say that he brought the same conviction in the triumph of spiritual power over human fear to the later stages of his career, including his campaigns against Pakistan's blasphemy laws and in favor of minority rights.

It was around this time that Bhatti first came to know a man who would become a mentor and source of inspiration throughout his career: Group Captain Cecil Chaudhry, a fighter pilot and military hero in the country who had served with distinction in the Indo-Pakistani war of 1965 and then as a squadron leader in the Indo-Pakistani war of 1971. He was awarded Pakistan's Star of Courage, roughly equivalent to the US Silver Star, for a particularly dangerous mission he led in the 1965 conflict.

A Catholic from a distinguished family, Chaudhry entered the Pakistani Air Force Academy in 1958 and received a double degree in aeronautics and mechanical engineering. After his military career was over, he entered academic life, serving as the principal of two different Catholic institutions before retiring in 2011. He died in April 2012 after a battle with lung cancer and was posthumously awarded the country's Pride of Performance Award by then-President Asif Ali Zadari.

Having felt he'd spent his entire life in service to the nation, Chaudhry chafed against what he saw as the second-class citizenship to which he and his fellow Christians in Pakistan were often consigned. A patriot, he was also alarmed by what he saw as a growing tendency toward radicalization in the country and the splintering of Pakistani society along confessional, class, and ethnic lines. He became active in the Punjab Education Foundation, working for the betterment of educational opportunities available to minority children, including not only religious minorities but also children with disabilities. After his death, his daughter Michelle founded the Cecil & Iris Chaudhry Foundation to continue his work on behalf of minority rights in Pakistan. A street in Lahore that runs past a Catholic school he once led is now named in his honor.

Bhatti first met Chaudhry in 1992, when his Christian Liberation Front was leading the first national campaign against Pakistan's blasphemy laws and the group wanted a personality with obvious patriotic appeal to help make the case. By all accounts, Bhatti was deeply impressed by Chaudhry's life story, as well as the fact that the war hero didn't simply cash in on his celebrity when his military career ended but rather reinvented himself as an educator and minority rights advocate, willing to put his popularity on the line to lend support to sometimes unpopular causes. He was also struck by Chaudhry's willingness to speak out at times in contrast with the wishes of his former colleagues and friends in the Pakistani military, some of whom clearly had links to elements among the more radical currents in the country's Islamic milieu.

Ten years after he came into Chaudhry's orbit, Shahbaz Bhatti had become an exceptionally mature thirty-four-year-old. By that stage he already carried two decades of experience of Pakistani politics as a minority rights activist, with a wide network of friends and allies thinking along the same lines in terms of the urgent need to defend the concept of a pluralistic and democratic society. Beginning as a devout young believer from a loving family and an idyllic Catholic environment in Khushpur, Bhatti's eyes had been opened early on to the realities of life for most impoverished and marginalized Christians in the country, and his instinctive activist streak, combined with his deep piety and his sense of destiny to lead, acquired from his father, positioned him as the ideal figure to do something big on a national scale.

That "something big" came in 2002 with the launch of the All-Pakistan Minorities Alliance, the group that would propel him to national prominence, make him a candidate for a federal minister's position within a government he had essentially shamed into action, and would eventually represent the cause for which he gave his life. To understand why the All-Pakistan Minorities Alliance is the point upon which Bhatti's story pivots, however, one needs to grasp a bit more about the situation facing religious minorities, especially Christians, in this overwhelmingly Muslim society that has become in some ways a safe harbor for Islamic terror groups. That's the subject of the next chapter.

CHAPTER TWO

Christians in Pakistan

Although Christians are one of the two largest religious minorities in Pakistan, along with Hindus, they're nevertheless an extremely small presence by comparative standards. At fewer than 3 million people, roughly evenly divided between Catholics and Protestants, they're less than 2 percent of the overall national population of 195 million. Hindus constitute just more than 2.1 million people, in a country where between 95 and 98 percent of Pakistanis are Muslim. Most of those are Sunni Muslims, although there are also sizable Shi'a and Sufi communities.

Christians in Pakistan are fond of tracing their origins back to the earliest church, usually through the missionary efforts of St. Thomas the Apostle, believed to have planted Christian communities in the late first century as far east as the Parthian Empire, in modern-day Iran, and inside India. According to tradition, St. Thomas evangelized the Indo-Pakistan subcontinent for thirty-two years and was martyred in AD 72. By the early third century, there were Christian bishops in northwest India, Afghanistan, and Baluchistan, which included parts of Iran, Afghanistan, and

Pakistan. In terms of the Catholic presence, Jesuit missionaries were active in Pakistan from the late sixteenth century, dispatched from their stronghold in Portuguese-held Goa in India. The Jesuits built a church in Lahore, the capital of Punjab, in 1596, after being granted permission by the emperor of the time, though that church was later destroyed and the Jesuit mission was suppressed in 1672.

Small pockets of Christians held on through the centuries in territories belonging to present-day Pakistan, alternatively tolerated or persecuted by the various powers, including emperors, Islamic dynasties, and later Sikh rule and even British colonization. The current physiognomy of the church in Pakistan, however, is largely a product of the missionary ferment of the late nineteenth century, when both Protestant and Catholic missionaries accompanying colonizing forces from Portugal, France, and Great Britain moved into the area.

The first Anglican bishop of Pakistan was appointed in 1877, while the first Roman Catholic diocese in the country, in Lahore, was erected in 1886 and trusted to the Capuchin order in 1888. Those European missionaries won relatively small numbers of converts, often drawn either from the elite ranks of Pakistanis serving in the army or the colonial-controlled government, or from the lowest social and economic classes who hoped to find in Christianity a route to emancipation. The largest Catholic jurisdiction in Pakistan is Lahore, reflecting Punjab's reputation as the Christian stronghold of the country.

Catholic missionaries from Belgium carried out much of the original missionary work in Punjab in the late nineteenth century, as chronicled in a thesis written by Emmanuel Masih at Rome's Gregorian University in 2011. He notes that before the arrival of European Christian missionaries, the religious landscape of Punjab was dominated by Islam,

Hinduism, and Sikhism, but much of the native population was considered outcast and untouchable so hadn't really been touched by any of those faiths. The Capuchins, Masih says, decided to make those groups its target audience.

However noble it may seem to Western Catholics, the choice to work for social justice and the idea of a "preferential option for the poor" have been chronic sources of controversy for the Catholic Church in Pakistan and other parts of the world, where resentful members of rival religions have accused missionaries of generating "rice Christians" with offers of food, education, medical care, employment, and so on. While no doubt there were abuses along those lines over the years, for the most part those charges have been off the mark, since the vast majority of beneficiaries of the Catholic Church's social service efforts in Pakistan, both historically and now, have not been Christian converts but rather Muslims.

The first Catholic missionaries arrived with British forces who entered Punjab in the period 1840–1845, building a number of chapels in the area that were largely designed for the pastoral care of Catholic members of the military and the colonial infrastructure. By the late 1880s, a number of Italian Capuchin missionaries were active in Punjab under British protection, but for some reason they ran afoul of the Vatican's missionary department, then known as Propaganda Fidei, and the decision came down that they were to be replaced. Responsibility was passed to their Belgian confreres in 1889, who would become the real founders of the Catholic presence in Pakistan. From essentially zero Catholics in 1889, by 1975 when the Belgian Capuchins withdrew, the Catholic population had grown to 175,000.

While many Protestant missionaries of the day had what one might call a trickle-down philosophy, aiming to convert the higher-class Brahmins in the conviction that the lower classes would follow, the Belgian Capuchins took a more bottom-up approach and enjoyed strong initial success—so much so, in fact, Masih reports that one well-known Protestant evangelist of the day was so impressed he himself actually converted. The Capuchins opened schools, founded agricultural settlements, created orphanages, and trained catechists, setting a pattern for the Catholic presence in Pakistan that endures to this day, with an emphasis on social service and empowerment of the lower classes, often enjoying the greatest missionary success among the poor and marginalized. Supposedly, Catholic priests also had a reputation for a less demanding *chanda*, or tithe, than their Protestant counterparts.

Unlike many Hindus during the era of partition with India, relatively few Christians fled Pakistan before the division between the two countries became official in 1947. Though it may seem ironic today, many Christians supported the independence drive led by Muhammad Ali Jinnah's All-India Muslim League. Influential Christians served as spokespeople and advocates for Jinnah, who is revered today by Pakistanis as the "Father of the Nation," and whose initial agenda included equality of citizenship and full protection of minority rights. Bhatti was actually a great admirer of Jinnah and often described his own advocacy for minority rights in terms of recovering the founder's original vision for the country.

The dream of an essentially secular Pakistan founded on citizenship rather than religious identity, however, quickly gave way to pressures for what today would be called Islamization. Pakistan officially declared itself an Islamic Republic in 1956, making Islam the basis for all legislation and the cornerstone of national identity. Still, no one was ever prosecuted for blasphemy in Pakistan until the era of President Muhammad Zia-ul-Haq in the late 1970s and 1980s, and several Christians played prominent roles in national life despite their minority status. One well-known Catholic example is Sr. Ruth Pfau, sometimes called the "Mother Teresa of Pakistan," a German missionary nun who spent most of her life in Pakistan battling leprosy. She is credited with being a large part of the reason that the World Health Organization declared Pakistan the first nation in Asia to have the disease largely under control. Pfau was awarded one of the country's highest civilian honors for her work in 1969 and was even granted Pakistani citizenship in 1988.

Despite its small size, the Catholic Church in Pakistan punches above its weight due to its extensive network of social service institutions, including running 534 schools, 53 hostels, 8 colleges, 7 technical institutes, and scores of healthcare clinics, centers for the elderly, orphanages, and hospitals. While the overwhelmingly majority of Pakistanis may be Muslim, a striking share of the population, especially among well-educated elites in the business, political, and academic worlds, have had extensive contact with the Catholic Church through its institutions. Caritas, the official Catholic charity in Pakistan, is also estimated to serve about 500,000 people every year, the vast majority of them Muslim.

To date, the Catholic Church in Pakistan has had only one cardinal: Cardinal Joseph Cordiero of Karachi, who was named an archbishop under St. Pope John XXIII in 1958 and elevated to the College of Cardinals by Blessed Pope Paul VI in 1973. Often mentioned as a *papabile*, or candidate to become pope, Cordiero represented a highwater mark for the visibility and prestige of Pakistan's Catholic leadership.

Second-class Citizenship

Aasiya Noreen Bibi, better known to the world as Asia Bibi, is likely the most famous, illiterate Punjabi farmworker and mother of five on the planet. She's the classic exception that proves the rule—the rare celebrity victim of the global war on Christians, in a universe of folks whose suffering typically unfolds under the cover of neglect. Bibi first became known in June 2009 when she was arrested and charged with the offense of blasphemy under Pakistani law. As she would later describe it, the dispute began when Bibi, a Catholic who regularly attended the Church of St. Teresa in the nearby town of Sheikhupura, was harvesting berries in scorching 100-degree heat to support her family. She became thirsty and drank from a well in her small village, thereby defiling the water source in the eyes of local Muslim women. As things escalated, she and some of the Muslim women began trading barbs about Jesus and Muhammad. Although Bibi insisted she meant no disrespect, the other women used her words as a pretext to whip up outrage and have her arrested.

Bibi remained in jail while an investigation and trial unfolded, which ended with her being sentenced to death by hanging in November 2010. To add insult to injury, she was also fined 300,000 Pakistani rupees, the equivalent of about $3,000, a staggering sum by rural standards. If the death sentence were to be carried out, she would become the first woman to be executed under the country's blasphemy law. Against all odds, Bibi's fate aroused fairly deep feelings around the world. The case went viral and has become a cause célèbre in Christian activist circles around the world. Documentaries have been made about Bibi, concerts organized in support of her, websites and twitter campaigns mobilized, books published, and petitions with hundreds of thousands of signatures have been delivered to the Pakistani authorities.

Despite three separate appeals of her death sentence, as of this writing Bibi remains in solitary confinement in a Pakistani prison, having spent her seventh consecutive Christmas behind bars. Pakistan's supreme court adjourned her death row appeal on October 13, 2016, after one of the three judges recused himself from the case, and it's unclear when the high court may resume its deliberations. Her family hopes an international pressure campaign will eventually see her freed, but in the meantime, one mullah in Pakistan has offered a reward of roughly $10,000 to anyone who kills her, either inside the prison or outside. That's a princely sum by Pakistani standards, enough to purchase a three-room house with all the modern conveniences. The mullah might well find a taker if Bibi doesn't make it out of the country first; according to one survey, at least 10 million Pakistanis say they would be willing to kill Bibi with their bare hands, either out of religious conviction, for the money, or both.

"I was a good wife, a good mother, and a good Christian," Bibi said. "Now it seems I'm only good to hang."

That comment came in a 2011 book titled *Blasphemy: The True, Heartbreaking Story of the Woman Sentenced to Death over a Cup of Water*, which was written clandestinely with a French journalist who passed questions to Bibi's husband, Ashiq, and then waited for hours outside the prison gates to collect Bibi's answers, relying on the help of an Urdu-English interpreter.

The Kafkaesque situation facing Asia Bibi captures in agonizing form the broader drama of Christianity in Pakistan. Despite its deep roots in the country and significant contributions to national life, Christianity is often seen as fatally "other" by the burgeoning nationalist and extremist movements in the country that are often interlinked with elements in politics, the military and security services, and the judiciary. That toxic combination makes life forever precarious for the Christian minority.

That's nowhere more clear than in application of the blasphemy laws that have been at the heart of the Asia Bibi prosecution. According to an analysis by the Pew Research Center's Forum on Religion & Public Life, nearly half the countries in the world, 47 percent, have laws or policies that criminalize apostasy, blasphemy, or defamation of religion. Anti-apostasy and anti-blasphemy laws tend to be most common in the Middle East, North Africa, and the Asia-Pacific. In the eyes of critics, they usually function to penalize religious minorities at the expense of whatever the socially dominant religious tradition may be, and Christians are not the only victims. In India a man who describes himself as a religious skeptic found himself facing blasphemy charges in 2012 because he claimed a statue of Jesus venerated by Mumbai's Catholic community for its miraculous qualities is a fake. In Greece, a man was arrested and charged with blasphemy around the same time after he posted satirical references to an Orthodox Christian monk on Facebook.

In Pakistan the victims of the blasphemy laws are disproportionately Christian. Although a criminal statute on blasphemy has been on the books since 1927, it was rarely used. In the 1980s, however, a definition of blasphemy seen by critics as arbitrary and vague was inserted into Section 295-C of the Pakistan Penal Code, and punishment was increased from two years of imprisonment to the death sentence for anyone convicted of blaspheming Muhammad. Under the revised law, the defiling of the Holy Qur'an is punishable with life imprisonment, defiling the name of the

Holy Prophet with death and defiling other important Quranic personages, with three years' imprisonment.

The United States Commission on International Religious Freedom has identified the uneven application of blasphemy laws in various countries, including Pakistan, as a serious problem.

"Blasphemy laws inappropriately position governments as arbiters of truth or religious rightness, as they empower officials to enforce particular religious views against individuals, minorities, and dissenters," the commission wrote in 2014. "In practice, they have proven to be ripe for abuse and easily manipulated with false accusations," the body's briefing paper said.

Examples abound. In 2012 a fourteen-year-old Christian girl named Rimsha Masih, who comes from an impoverished family of sweepers, was charged with blasphemy after accusations were made that she had torn pages out of a Muslim textbook used to teach the Qur'an. Relatives and human rights workers claimed that the girl has Down syndrome and should therefore be exempt; the charges were eventually dismissed. In the meantime, however, her family went into hiding out of fear for their physical safety.

In mid-January 2013 there were even efforts to charge Pakistan's ambassador to the United States, Sherry Rehman, under the blasphemy laws on the basis of a television interview she gave in 2010 that some Muslims felt was disrespectful to Muhammad. Muhammad Faheem Ahkter Gill, a thirty-one-year-old businessman who owns a marble business in the city of Multan, drove the case against Rehman. A court directed police to investigate, though no charges were filed, while Rehman, a member of the leftist People's Party, claimed she had already faced death threats over her public opposition to the blasphemy laws.

Yet blasphemy charges are hardly the only threats Christians face in Pakistan. A 2009 anti-Christian atrocity in the town of Gojra, in Punjab province, is emblematic of the chronic risk of physical violence even in the absence of judicial cover for it. Seven members of a Christian family, including two children and three women, were burned alive by a frenzied Muslim mob after rumors had circulated that pages from a Qur'an had been burned during a Christian wedding the week before. Clerics in local mosques reportedly laced their sermons that week with anti-Christian rhetoric, inspiring a mob estimated at 20,000 people to storm Gojra's Christian colony. They met some resistance from the Christians, but eventually they picked a house more or less at random, shot dead a family elder, and then set the home ablaze when the rest of the members of the family barricaded themselves inside. Although a hundred other homes were also torched, there were no other reports of fatalities. Various government officials expressed outrage, but an official investigation did not result in any prosecutions.

Over the years, Christians in Pakistan have also been frequent targets for bomb attacks. At Christmastime in 1998, for instance, a bomb exploded at the historic St. Patrick's Cathedral in Karachi, originally built in 1845 and one of the largest Christian worship spaces in the country. Such acts of anti-Christian violence in Pakistan have become depressingly commonplace. Here's an incomplete sampling of events over the last decade.

- In October 2001 a gunman on a motorcycle opened fire on a Protestant congregation in the Punjab, killing eighteen people.

- In March 2002 five Christians were killed in an attack on a church in Islamabad, including an American schoolgirl and her mother.

- In August 2002 masked gunmen stormed a Christian missionary school in Islamabad, leaving six people dead and three more injured.

- Also in August 2002 grenades were tossed at a church on the grounds of a Christian hospital in northwestern Pakistan, killing three nurses.

- On September 25, 2002, two terrorists entered a Christian peace and justice institute in Karachi, where they proceeded to separate the Muslims from the Christians and then murdered seven of the Christians by shooting them in the head. The hands of the victims had been tied behind their backs and their mouths covered with tape.

- On Christmas Day 2002 radicals tossed a hand grenade into a church near Lahore, leaving three young girls dead in the blast.

- In November 2005 some 3,000 Muslim radicals assaulted Catholic, Salvation Army, and United Presbyterian churches in Sangla Hill, supposedly in response to violation of the blasphemy laws by a young Christian man. Dozens of people were injured in the attacks.

- In June 2006 a Pakistani Christian stonemason was working near Lahore when he reportedly drank water from a public facility and was assaulted by a group of Muslims who called him a "Christian dog." The man was hospitalized for injuries sustained during the beating.

- In August 2007 a Christian missionary couple, Rev. Arif Khan and Kathleen Khan, were gunned down by Islamic radicals in Islamabad. Authorities said that Khan had been killed over accusations of sexual abuse lodged by a member of his congregation, but local Christians disputed that account.

- In November 2011 an eighteen-year-old Catholic girl named Amarish Masih was murdered in her small village near Faisalabad, allegedly because she refused the advances of a local Muslim man. No charges were filed in the incident, which is not uncommon in Pakistan, where rape victims are sometimes imprisoned for unlawful sex and released only on the condition that they marry the rapist.

- On December 26, 2011, a young Christian man near Lahore was arrested and imprisoned over the charge of blasphemy, allegedly because he burned pages of the Qur'an to prepare tea. The man said the charge was actually a pretext, arising from a rent dispute with his Muslim landlord. An angry Muslim crowd formed outside the man's house and threatened other Christians living in the area.

- Also in late December 2011, a pregnant Christian woman and her husband were arrested by police and charged with theft on the basis of complaints by local Muslims. The couple complained of being beaten while in police custody, and the woman, Salma Emmanuel, aged thirty, was hospitalized for life-threatening injuries both to herself and to her unborn child. Her husband, a TV repairman, said police told him the beating would stop if he agreed to convert to Islam.

- In March 2013 Muslims attacked a Christian neighborhood in Lahore, where more than 100 houses were burned after a Christian was alleged to have made blasphemous remarks.

- On September 22, 2013, 127 people were killed and some 250 injured in twin suicide bombing attacks on the historic All Saints Church located in the old quarter of the city of Pewshawar, in what at the time stood as the single deadliest attack on the country's Christian minority. A group called Jundallah, an offshoot of the Pakistani Taliban, asserted responsibility for the attack, saying that Christians are "enemies of Islam" and vowing that terror attacks would continue until US drone strikes in Pakistan ended.

- On March 15, 2015, two bomb blasts erupted at a Catholic parish and another Christian church in the Youhanabad neighborhood of Lahore during Sunday services, leaving at least fifteen people dead and more than seventy wounded. Pope Francis condemned those attacks while leading a prayer during the Easter season, calling it a "cowardly and senseless crime."

- On March 27, 2016, which was Easter day that year, at least 70 people were killed and more than 340 wounded when a suicide bomber detonated himself in a Lahore park in a predominantly Christian area where people were celebrating the Easter holiday. The Pakistani Taliban claimed responsibility for the assault.

- Also in 2016 a study by the United States Commission on International Religious Freedom found "deeply troubling content" in the way public school textbooks in Pakistan depict non-Islamic faiths, especially Christians and Hindus, styling them as "nefarious, violent, and tyrannical by nature," in what the authors of the study described as a classic example of "public shaming."

- In September 2016 Pakistani police arrested a sixteen-year-old Christian boy on blasphemy charges after he "liked" an inappropriate photograph on Facebook of the Kaaba in Mecca, one of the holiest sites in Islam. Police sources stated they made the arrest after being alerted of the Facebook post by a Muslim, who said he found it insulting.

Unfortunately, this catalog of misery and atrocities has become so numbingly familiar as to barely rate any mention in global news reports, but they're in the minds of Christian families in Pakistan every time they go to worship services, drop their children off at a church-sponsored school, patronize a Christian-owned business, or simply walk down the streets. Some Christians in Pakistan have drawn the conclusion that the faith has no long-term future in the country, feeling that it's being gradually squeezed out with basic legal and political impunity, if not outright encouragement.

The 2015 church bombings in Lahore prompted Pope Francis to make one of his most anguished public statements on anti-Christian persecution to date. "These are Christian churches. Christians are persecuted, our brothers spill their blood simply because they are Christians," the pontiff said after his regular Sunday Angelus address. Francis continued, "I pray to the Lord that the persecution against Christians, that the world is trying to hide, comes to an end. Let there be peace!"

While some of the incidents listed above are recent, by the year 2002 similar acts of violence and intimidation had already become routine, leaving scars in the Christian psyche in Pakistan that have only deepened with time. This was the landscape coming into view on July 14, 2002, when Shahbaz Bhatti was the driving force behind convening the All-Pakistan Minorities Convention in Islamabad, which in turn generated the cause that would become his life's work. The organization, All-Pakistan Minorities Alliance, would propel him into public office and also make him public enemy number one for Pakistan's radical Islamic factions.

CHAPTER THREE

All-Pakistan Minorities Alliance

If Shahbaz Bhatti had done nothing with his life beyond standing up for the persecuted Christians of Pakistan, that alone would be enough to make him a hero and perhaps even a saint. After all, he did so knowing full well that he was risking his life. Beginning early on he suffered harassment, beatings, and even torture, but he was not deterred. His concept of what it meant to defend Christians included encouraging them to express the Gospel in concrete acts of service despite the threats they faced, such as his efforts to have his youth group at the university in Lahore raise money for scholarships so poorer Christians could continue their studies or the celebrated account of his rescuing a trapped family during a Punjabi flood.

Yet the compelling appeal of the Bhatti story is that precisely because he was so intensely concerned with his own minority group in Pakistan, he could easily appreciate how others would be equally concerned with theirs. In that sense he was a classic example of the St. John Paul II principle: he could be universal precisely because he was ineradicably particular. John Paul II was Polish down to his toes, as loyal and romantic a son as Poland ever produced, and because of that, he could connect with the love of place, people, and culture that he found everywhere in the world.

In Bhatti's case that transition from the particular to the universal, at least in an external sense, can be dated with some precision. It first became visible on July 14, 2002, in Islamabad, Pakistan's national capital, when Bhatti convened the first All-Pakistan Minorities Convention, a gathering of Christians, Hindus, Ahmadis, Sufis, and other minority groups, as well as NGOs and members of parliament, to come together to adopt a common platform in favor of democracy, the rule of law, and the protection of basic human rights. It marked the first time in the history of Pakistan that representatives of all the country's minority groups had come together under one roof, and the assembly ended with the decision to create a permanent organization, the All-Pakistan Minorities Alliance (APMA), and the unanimous choice of Bhatti as chairman.

The new chairman explained the purpose of the organization at the time:

> The main aim of the formation of APMA is to forge unity among the religious minorities of Pakistan so that, from a common and single platform, peaceful struggle could be launched to secure, preserve, protect and promote the religious, social, economic and political rights of minority groups. It is mandatory upon APMA to enhance the understanding of human rights, to propagate democratic norms and to assist in alleviating extremism, countering the tendency of dividing the Pakistani nation on the basis of religion, and struggling to accelerate efforts to build a better democratic and progressive Pakistan according to the ideals of our founding father, Quaid-e-Azam Mohammad Ali Jinnah.

Right out of the gate, the new organization had its work cut out for it. Following the terrorist attacks of September 11, 2001, the US-led invasion of Afghanistan had forced leaders in the region to take sides. Then-Pakistani President Pervez Musharraf chose to join the US-led coalition in going to war against the Taliban, enraging extremist Muslim sentiment in the country and triggering a series of attacks on Christian targets up and down Pakistan. Bhatti was among the voices crying the most loudly for protection. Quoted in his new capacity as leader of the All-Pakistan Minorities Alliance, he told the Reuters news agency in August 2002: "If immediate steps are not taken by authorities to provide protection to Christians, I fear that it will lead to the start of genocide in Pakistan. We will definitely stage protests. We will not remain silent."

Truer words were never spoken, as Bhatti was not someone inclined either by conviction or temperament to go quietly into that good night.

In his 2005 interview with Monsignor Dino Pistolato, Bhatti recalled that at the beginning of the alliance, he and his friends from the Christian Liberation Front, who helped form the nucleus of the new group, "travelled long distances on foot, by bus and by bicycle to reach people a bit everywhere to help the suffering Christians and to pray with them. The message delivered was they were not alone, but a part of our family. From village to village, from town to town, from city to city, we united the Christians on one platform . . . to become one family, to share each other's sufferings and sorrow, [and] to support each other and glorify the Lord's name in this country."

To be clear, the efforts of the alliance to expose discrimination and double standards, combined with Bhatti's outspokenness, always exposed it to risk. For instance in

September 2002, two gunmen entered the Institute for Peace and Justice in Karachi and killed seven people by shooting them point-blank in the head. All the victims were Pakistani Christians. Although the gunmen were never arrested or prosecuted, when members of the All-Pakistan Minorities Alliance organized a public protest in Karachi, several members were arrested and jailed on charges of disturbing the public peace.

Whenever an act of brutality against Christians or members of another minority would explode, Bhatti's alliance was always there to speak up, generally doing so more quickly and loudly than other activist groups. In April 2003, for instance, some valuable law books went missing from the municipal building of Sanda, located on the outskirts of Lahore, and two Christian janitors were jailed while ten Muslim clerks, secretaries, and other office staff with direct access to the books were neither interrogated nor detained. The two Christians were held in police custody for twenty days, after which one of them was admitted to the hospital, reportedly from beatings he had suffered in custody, and eventually died. In an ensuing protest a relative of the man who was struck over the head by a police baton also suffered a fatal injury. The All-Pakistan Minorities Alliance registered a formal compliant, asking for the police involved to be charged. No action was ever taken, though the widow of the original victim was eventually given compensation equivalent to roughly $2,000, which, as Bhatti ruefully observed at the time, seemed to be the price tag for a Christian life in Pakistan.

True to the alliance's vision, Bhatti didn't speak out only when Christians were attacked, but whenever members of other minority groups found themselves in the firing line as well. In October 2005, for instance, eight people were killed and twenty injured when radical Islamic gunmen opened fire on a mosque of the Ahmadiyya, a movement within Islam founded in Punjab in the late nineteenth century that was officially declared heretical in Pakistan by a constitutional amendment in 1974. Bhatti told the BBC at the time that the All-Pakistan Minorities Alliance condemned the act, adding that he also saw it as part of a systematic failure on the part of Pakistan's government to provide security for minority groups and to protect their rights.

Similarly, when a suicide bombing ripped through the fabled Bari Imam Shrine in Islamabad in May 2005 during a festival for Shi'a Muslims, Bhatti forcefully denounced the attack as "a barbaric act, a great tragedy and a heinous crime against humanity. . . . This violent act was committed by those elements who wanted to destabilize Pakistan with their devilish designs. No religion allows the killings of innocent people," he said, adding that "such elements deserved no mercy," and offered condolences to the victims and their families on behalf of all of Pakistan's religious minorities, once again insisting that the government "invite all mainstream political and religious parties on this issue and formulate an effective strategy to curb growing terrorism and suicide attacks."

In 2006 Bhatti publicly warned of what he saw as a worrying trend of Hindus abandoning Pakistan, most heading across the border to neighboring India—a result, he charged, of Pakistan's failure to protect their rights. He said things had been deteriorating for Pakistan's Hindu minority ever since the 1992 destruction of the famous mosque Babri Masjid in Uttar Pradesh, India, at the hands of Hindu radicals, which triggered a spate of reprisal attacks in Pakistan.

Bhatti also had a clear-eyed understanding that although Pakistan is an overwhelmingly Muslim nation, under the right circumstances even majority Sunni Muslims too could easily become the victims of religious persecution and human rights violations, generally because they have a more moderate understanding of Islam and defy the claims of the radicals to be the legitimate representatives of the faith. On his watch the APMA compiled statistics released in 2006 showing that from 1985 to 2004 there had been 601 prosecutions under the blasphemy laws in Pakistan, of which 295 were against Muslims, putting them in first place, followed by 203 against Ahmadis, 79 against Christians, and 24 against Hindus. Aside from demonstrating the common exposure of all religious groups, Bhatti was also making a savvy political point by trumpeting those numbers—he was warning the country's majority that the mere fact of being Muslim is no insulation against feeling the sting of persecution.

Also in 2005 the All-Pakistan Minorities Alliance led a coalition of various minority groups and human rights NGOs to oppose a move by the government to reinstitute a religion column on national passports, requiring Pakistani citizens to declare their religious affiliation, which critics saw as a pretext for additional discrimination. In a statement Bhatti called the idea "unfortunate and devoid of any logic, reason or civilized norm. It only shows that the government has once again buckled under the pressure of religious extremists. A passport is not a certificate of religious belief, it only certifies the nationality of [a] holder."

Going on Offense

Bhatti wasn't content for his new organization merely to play defense, reacting to incidents of violence and intimidation as they occurred. He also wanted the All-Pakistan Minorities Alliance to go on the offensive, campaigning for an essentially secular state that would not impose religious belief as a condition of full citizenship. In particular that meant strenuous opposition to various forms of Islamization that had been gathering steam in Pakistan since the Zia years, including pressure for the adoption of sharia in various zones of the country, the increasing use of blasphemy laws to harass and intimidate minorities, and the adoption of "Hudood laws" beginning in 1977, making adultery and fornication criminal offenses and assigning traditional Islamic punishments such as whipping, amputation, and stoning to death. In practice the ordinances are seen as strongly discriminatory against women, and the pressure brought by Bhatti's alliance is one reason they were amended in 2006 through adoption of a Women's Protection Bill.

Throughout his career Bhatti was sensitive to the fact that discrimination against minorities in Pakistan often overlapped with discrimination against women, in part because of the impress of Islamic law which, depending on the school and the interpretation, often disadvantages women, and in part because women often are especially vulnerable and powerless to protest mistreatment. As a result women became a focus of concern and one of the categories of minorities in the country with which he was especially concerned.

In addition to legal and political crusades, Bhatti also wanted the All-Pakistan Minorities Alliance to be a support and relief group for the victims of religious persecution, as he explained in 2005:

> APMA extended practical support to the victims of these unjust laws, particularly those of the blasphemy law, forced conversion, rape and hateful crimes. Medical, financial and legal aid has been provided to them, and efforts have been

made to provide relief and to stop such heinous crimes. The families of these victims also suffer enormously and face threats. In these conditions, the families are shifted to safer places and supported until they are out of danger. APMA has helped many Christian women who have been abducted, tortured, raped, and forcefully converted to Islam. Free legal aid, rehabilitation and settlement are proved to assure them of the love of Christ . . . many girls have been saved and helped to overcome their traumatic experiences and to lead dignified lives.

Similarly, APMA mobilized to provide humanitarian relief for the victims of violent attacks against minority groups, such as bombings of Christian churches or Ahmadi mosques. "On many occasions, we were the first to arrive and to assist the victims, the wounded and the victims' families," Bhatti recalled. "We gave support in the rehabilitation of the churches. We strongly raised our voice, but we also practically helped the attacked churches, the wounded and the families of the martyrs. We are still supporting the victims' families, especially those who have lost their heads of household. Whenever anything happens, any act of violence or terrorism, anything, we reach out and help the people immediately."

As APMA's work evolved, legal aid became one strong subspecialty. A typical case arose in 2006, when a Muslim man in the Punjabi city of Sialkot kidnapped the Christian woman he employed to clean his house along with her thirteen-year-old daughter, holding them for months and subjecting them to torture in an effort to force them to convert to Islam. The mother and daughter had become domestic servants after the family's husband, who ran a poultry breeding farm, got sick with bird flu and died. The case only came to light after three months, when a relative came to see the mother and daughter and was chased away.

She contacted the APMA, who filed a legal brief with the Lahore high court. The court in turn instructed a bailiff to go to the home, and the two women were freed. The APMA also sought prosecutions against the Muslim couple, but no action was taken. As Bhatti said, "The growing victimization of Christians and minorities in general is alarming. We try to help the families of victims and at the same time, to find legal and practical channels to help those submitted to such violence, but the government must intervene forcefully to stop them."

"A Place at Jesus' Feet"

As Bhatti's national profile grew during this period, and as the APMA demonstrated a track record of success in effectively shaming the government into at least limited and reluctant action to protect minority rights, Bhatti attracted the attention of forces in the country alarmed at his mounting influence. The first strategy they attempted, he would later recount, was the time-honored gambit of co-opting one's enemies, essentially seeking to buy him off. He was offered high government positions and various sinecures if he would abandon his struggle, but he said, "I always refused to give up, even at the cost of my life."

"I do not want popularity," he said. "I do not want any position. I just want a place at Jesus' feet," a line that would go on to be among Bhatti's most-quoted sayings.

Because one of the tests for sainthood is the extent to which a given candidate's actions were driven specifically by the Catholic faith, and not political or generic humanitarian aims, it's important to allow Bhatti to speak for himself about the motives that drove his activism with the APMA.

"I want that my life, my character, and my actions speak for me and indicate that I am following Jesus Christ. Because of this desire, I will consider myself even to be more fortunate if—in this effort and struggle to help the needy, the poor, to help the persecuted and victimized Christians of Pakistan—Jesus Christ will accept the sacrifice of my life. I want to live for Christ, and I want to die for him." These words were uttered six full years before Bhatti was killed in March 2011.

"I am very much inspired by the Holy Bible and the life of Jesus Christ," he said. "The more I read from the New and Old Testaments, verses from the Holy Bible, the Word of God, the more it gives strength and determination. When I see that Jesus Christ sacrificed everything, and that our Lord sent his son for our redemption and salvation, I ask myself how I can follow the path to Calvary. I know that our Lord said, 'Come to me, hold your Cross, and follow the path.'"

Likewise, Bhatti said that his perennial drive to link his defense of minority rights with concrete acts of service also were rooted in Scripture: "The verses I like the most from the Holy Bible read, 'You came to me when I was hungry, when I was thirsty, when I was imprisoned.' So when I see poor people, I think it might be Jesus coming to me. Hence I always try to help, along with my colleagues, those in need, the hungry and thirsty."

One will rarely find a clearer statement of religious motivation, what might look to the world as political or legal activism, than these statements from Shahbaz Bhatti.

When muzzling Bhatti through payoffs failed to throw him off the chase, he said that extremists then turned to issuing death threats to both him and other members of his family. At one point representatives of an extremist group visited his mother and father to warn them that if he didn't go quiet, they would lose their son. After the visit, Bhatti said his father encouraged him not to lose heart and to keep up the fight.

"Many times the extremists wanted to kill me, many times they wanted to put me in prison, they threatened me, they harassed me, and they terrorized my family," Bhatti recalled. He was also subjected to various forms of harassment and intimidation by the government, such as being placed on a national "Exit Control List" in 2003, a move that essentially made it impossible for him to travel abroad. Officials knew that Bhatti was becoming a celebrity in the human rights world and worried that foreign-speaking appearances and media interviews would contribute to a negative international perception of Pakistan.

Criticism

From the beginning, the APMA under Bhatti had a sharp political edge, which sometimes led critics to wonder if Bhatti himself may have been using the group to advance his own political ambitions, a charge that would dog him throughout his career and one he consistently denied.

One of Bhatti's first public battles after the alliance was founded came when then-President Pervez Musharraf amended the constitution to prevent former prime ministers from serving more than two terms, in effect banning opposition leader Benazir Bhutto, at the time living in exile in Dubai, from returning to power. Bhatti minced no words in denouncing the move as "a sheer violation of the law of the land."

"In order to continue the presidential dictatorship and give cover to unconstitutional acts, the military rulers are stopping the way of Benazir Bhutto, under whose leadership people have decided to build a better Pakistan," Bhatti said in a statement. Although Bhatti insisted he was siding with Bhutto only because she promised a better deal for the country's minorities, the sharply partisan tone of his rhetoric nevertheless troubled some APMA supporters, including a few members of the Catholic hierarchy, who wondered if it might make things worse for Christians in the country by linking them too explicitly with a specific political option.

In fact in 2003 there was an internal uprising within the Christian Liberation Front that Bhatti had founded, which announced that he had been ousted as chairman due to his excessive ties to Bhutto's Pakistan People's Party and that new leadership had been installed—ironically, under former member of parliament Simon Jacob Gill, a fellow native son of Khushpur. A statement issued by the new leadership, presented at a press conference attended by Punjab's then-chief minister, Chaudhry Pervaz Elahi, who belongs to the rival Pakistan Muslim League, asserted that Bhatti had "lost confidence among CLF members with his undue following of the Pakistan People's Party" and that what had occurred was a "revolution in the CLF to end the one-man rule of the ex-chairman."

Unintimidated, Bhatti continued to be an explicit opponent of Musharraf and an open supporter of the People's Party. In May 2007 when armed bands seen as proxies for pro-Musharraf forces attacked a People's Party rally in Karachi, Bhatti issued a statement in the name of the APMA, saying that the "government deliberately stoked the violence against political parties."

Another fine line Bhatti had to walk over the years was not getting too far ahead of opinion within his Christian base, even when it cut against the pro-democracy and freedom of expression agenda of his own alliance. One such case arose in 2006, when many Christians in Pakistan decided that for once the blasphemy laws should work for them rather than against them, successfully campaigning to compel the government to ban distribution in Pakistan of the movie *The Da Vinci Code*, a film that was controversial among Catholics in particular for its nefarious depiction of the Vatican and groups within the church such as Opus Dei. The country's then-minister of culture, Jalil Abbas, explained the decision by saying, "The film is sacrilegious to all religions, that's why we did this."

Bhatti was publicly supportive of the campaign to ban the film, saying at one stage, "*The DaVinci Code* is a sacrilegious act in the guise of freedom of expression and fiction." He also said that both the novel and the film "hurt the religious sentiments of Christians and Muslims throughout the world," suggesting that author Dan Brown had "evil intentions" and wanted "to undermine the historical as well as theological truth about Jesus Christ."

Critics, however, argued that it was hypocritical for Bhatti to be simultaneously campaigning for the complete abolition of Pakistan's blasphemy laws and also celebrating their application in a rare instance in which they seemed to support the confessional interests of his own Christian denomination.

The 2005 Earthquake

Whatever criticism Bhatti may have faced during the APMA years, it was always balanced against his growing reputation as a humanitarian. No moment better crystallized that aspect of Bhatti's career than the APMA's response to a devastating 7.6 magnitude earthquake that struck the northern Pakistani region of Kashmir, on the border with India, on October 8, 2005, leaving an estimated 87,000 people dead, 75,000 injured, and a staggering 2.8 million people displaced. According to *Live Science*, it was the fifteenth deadliest earthquake in history, and it struck a largely impoverished region ill-equipped to deal with the fallout.

As initial reports of the disaster began to come in, Bhatti immediately mobilized APMA members and set off for Balakot, a town of 30,000 people in northwestern Pakistan that was completely destroyed, setting up base camps there for relief efforts. Bhatti later described the scene: "The roads were blocked, everywhere there were body parts, bodies and blood were spread everywhere. Balakot became like a graveyard, a city of dead bodies." It's worth noting that Balakot was a largely Muslim and Sikh settlement with no real Christian presence, although there was one hospital in the city at the time of the disaster run by a Pakistani Christian physician.

During the first week after the disaster, the APMA team went to work, initially helping rescue-and-security forces to dig dead bodies out of the rubble. Team members also climbed into the mountains surrounding Balakot, assisting with rescue operations and digging the dead out of the collapsed mountainsides. They transferred the injured to hospitals, they donated blood, they provided medicine to the injured, and they assisted the Pakistan army and international rescue teams. The APMA volunteers made a special point of trying to rescue and care for school-aged children who had lost their parents when the quake struck and who had no immediate family members nearby to take them in.

After a week, the APMA expanded its relief effort in Balakot to try to provide for the longer-term needs of the injured and displaced. Among other things, they distributed winterized tents they had purchased with donated funds from APMA supporters, as well as mattresses, jackets to fight the winter cold, and food and water. Overall, the

APMA estimates that in excess of 10,000 families benefited from their assistance in the first stages after the disaster.

By October 18, APMA was running a soup kitchen in Balakot that provided hot meals everyday to more than 5,000 people. That soup kitchen would remain in operation for more than a year, until December 2006. They also set up three tent villages in Balakot, Sanghar, and Neelam Valley, where roughly 2,000 families took up residence and were provided with medical facilities, food and water, and bedding. Next, APMA began to create "tent schools" across the disaster zone, where children who had lost their parents were able to continue their studies, which was in part a way of restoring some sense of normalcy to their lives.

"These students were traumatized," Bhatti said. "We gave them parental care, special care, so that they could feel somebody was there to help them, to give them love." He noted that more than 10,000 schools across the disaster zone had been destroyed, and that the earthquake was especially menacing for children because it struck in the morning when they were at school and separated from their families. In scores of cases, children either went home to find their homes destroyed and their families dead, or parents went to school to find their children, only to discover the school wiped out. In the end more than 1,000 students attended one of the tent schools operated by the APMA, the vast majority of them either Muslims or Sikhs.

"Especially in those days, when there was the smell of dead bodies, when nobody bothered to come and the biggest organizations were not ready to come, when people were wearing masks, we went there to serve the suffering, to help them, to tell them, 'We are with you,'" Bhatti said.

APMA maintained its presence well after the initial press for humanitarian relief was over, continuing to operate three schools in the area years later that provided 250 students with a free education as well as clothing, food, and health care. "The purpose," Bhatti said in 2005, "is to show generosity, kindness of heart, mercy, care and love that is consistent with the message of Christ."

Bhatti was active in soliciting support from abroad to help the earthquake victims, including from Caritas, the official Catholic charity in the Patriarchate of Venice. Through his efforts, Caritas in Venice promised to help rebuild 300 houses in the damage zone of the quake, to construct two schools, and also to assist with transportation and other needs. The housing element was especially important, given that the earthquake struck on the cusp of the typically brutal winter in the Kashmir region, and displaced persons found themselves living in unheated tents during periods of cold rain and snow.

The alliance's efforts did not go unnoticed. After the initial chaos of the relief campaign began to give way to longer-term efforts at reconstruction, the Pakistani army awarded the APMA a formal certificate of appreciation for its contributions. Ironically, the APMA over the four years of its existence at that point was among the leading national critics of the army, repeatedly faulting it for failing to provide adequate security for minority groups and also for discriminating against those minorities in its own ranks.

It may seem counterintuitive for an organization founded to campaign for minority rights to have invested so much of its time and treasure in what was essentially a humanitarian effort with no clear focus on minority groups, but Bhatti saw it differently:

> This earthquake is a big tragedy in Pakistan, but I think it also opened a door for the Christians and all those who

believe in humanity and touched the heart of many. Christians of the world who extended their hands to these Muslims and the affectees in need have built a bridge of solidarity, love, understanding, cooperation and tolerance between the two religions. If these efforts continue, I think that we will win the hearts and minds of the extremists. This will bring a positive change—people will not hate each other, will not kill in the name of religion, but they will love each other, they will bring harmony, they will cultivate peace and understanding in the region. I think the needy persons, the poor, the orphaned children, whatever their religion, should be considered human beings, God's creatures. We should love them and extend help to them.

With the benefit of hindsight, that forecast now seems overly optimistic, but it reflected the surge of national pride in Pakistan in 2005 when the country set aside its traditional sectarian divides and united in a common effort. Bhatti's conviction was that if the majority Muslims in the country saw minority groups stepping up in a moment of national need, they would come to understand that Christians, Ahmadis, Hindus, Sikhs, and others were not a foreign presence, but rather fellow Pakistanis ready to do their part.

Always, however, the spiritual element was foremost in Bhatti's understanding of the work to which he had been called.

"We believe this is a mission to help suffering humanity, to spread Jesus' love, to glorify his name," he said. It's "a mission to love our neighbors, to love people in need, the poor. I only want that God blesses us and gives us energy and resources so that we can be helping hands for these victims, the needy and poor people. We want to prove that we are following our Christ, who has given his life for us and died for us, who gave us salvation and a message of freedom, of hope, of salvation and redemption."

Ann Buwalda, founder of the Jubilee Campaign, a religious liberty advocacy group, witnessed Bhatti's effectiveness as the APMA leader when she visited Pakistan in 2005. "There was a village outside of Lahore where five churches were burnt to the ground in a rampage," she told *Christianity Today* in 2011. Within two days after the incident, Bhatti's group had posted signs on all five churches, "basically declaring that the Christian minority were in solidarity with those who had been persecuted."

"Every time you took a picture of the Presbyterian church that had been burnt to the ground, you also took a picture of Shahbaz Bhatti's organization's banner," Buwalda said. "He was a very smart advocate within Pakistan to get his name put forward, and that's an important factor when you're trying to influence a government that views a Christian as less than a citizen."

This was the profile of Shahbaz Bhatti by November 2008. He had developed a national and international reputation as a political activist and human rights champion. Despite some criticism and controversy, his leadership during the 2005 earthquake and the herculean efforts of the APMA in the disaster zone also marked him as a leading humanitarian and a figure willing to walk his own talk. In a moment of national crisis, therefore, he seemed a natural choice for a new government looking to give itself credibility both domestically and internationally, meaning that the stage was set for the next improbable chapter in the Bhatti story when he explicitly entered politics and became the first Christian ever to serve in a Pakistani cabinet.

CHAPTER FOUR

Minister for Minorities Affairs

In the abstract, when Bhatti became Pakistan's first-ever federal minister for minorities affairs in November 2008, it might seem a doubly anomalous development. For one thing, it meant placing a Christian in the cabinet in an overwhelmingly Muslim nation where Islam was constitutionally enshrined as the basis of national life and the Qu'ran recognized as the basis of all law, making it a deeply politically sensitive thing for any government to do.

For another, despite the fact that Bhatti's advocacy for minority rights often skirted the fine line between humanitarian concern and partisan politics, he had always insisted he never sought or would accept a government position. "I believe people can have wealth, money, positions, everything. . . . But the spiritual satisfaction I get through this work! I could not feel the same if I were given a million dollars! I am satisfied in this world," he said confidently, just three years before he changed course and decided to accept a government post after all.

To understand why Bhatti would make such an apparently self-contradictory choice, it is important to grasp where

Pakistan stood in 2008 and the unique moment of opportunity Bhatti clearly believed the country was experiencing.

Just eleven months before Bhatti went into government, Pakistan experienced a national trauma that was stunning, even by the grisly and often lethal standards of the country's history. On December 27, 2007, two-time former Prime Minister Benazir Bhutto, who had been the first woman to lead a majority Muslim nation and the only one to do it twice, was assassinated while leading a campaign rally for her left-leaning Pakistan People's Party. Gunmen opened fire on her car just as Bhutto had stood up through a sunroof to wave to the crowds and then detonated explosives in the area. An investigation by Scotland Yard would conclude in 2008 that Bhutto died as a result of blunt force trauma to the head caused by the bombs, rather than gunshot wounds. In the immediate aftermath of the attack, a Pakistani offshoot of Al-Qaeda claimed responsibility, although Bhutto's followers were convinced the assassination was actually orchestrated by then-President Pervez Musharraf, who resigned amid the ensuing scandal and went into exile in London. Courts would eventually indict Musharraf for an alleged role in the assassination, but he was never convicted or jailed.

Long a lightning rod, Bhutto and her family had been placed under house arrest following a 1977 military coup, and her father, former Prime Minister Zufikar Bhutto, was hanged in 1979 by the military regime under Muhammad Zia-ul-Haq. She then inherited leadership of the party, and when she wasn't in power she would spend much of the rest of her career in exile.

Though politics is always a shadowy business in which it's often difficult to separate the good guys from the bad, in broad strokes Bhutto and the People's Party represented the dream of an essentially secular, liberal state in Pakistan, as opposed to a more theocratic order based upon strict interpretations of Islamic law. At the same time, however, her administrations were also hobbled by accusations of nepotism and corruption, making her both an admired and also deeply controversial figure. A 1998 *New York Times* investigative report, for instance, traced more than 100 million in offshore assets to Bhutto and her family, including a 350-acre luxury estate in Surrey, England. Despite all that, for Bhatti and like-minded minority rights activists in the country, there was never any serious question that the platform the Bhuttos and the People's Party represented was the only choice for the country's future.

After Bhutto's death, her nineteen-year-old son, Bilawal Bhutto Zardari, took over as head of the Pakistani People's Party, a post he holds to this day. Bhutto's husband, Asif Ali Zardari, emerged from national elections in February 2008 as the new president of Pakistan, after returning from exile in Dubai following his wife's death. He was formally elected as the country's president in early September 2008, and among his first moves was to invite Bhatti to join the government.

It's important to appreciate the mood in Pakistan at the time in order to understand why Bhatti accepted the offer. Among moderates and secularists, there was a conviction that the Bhutto assassination had changed the national calculus. They believed that if even a legend such as Bhutto could be felled, the country perhaps would finally be ready to confront the extremist menace and embrace a new course. Further, with Bhutto no longer on the scene, they also felt optimistic that the scandals that had long surrounded the People's Party might be a thing of the past, and that Pakistan could take decisive steps forward toward becoming a pluralistic society in which minority rights would be better protected and the threat of imposing sharia or prosecuting innocents under the blasphemy laws could be consigned to the past.

That was the milieu in which Bhatti, who was just forty at the time, made the choice to enter government service on November 2, 2008. He said he was doing so for the sake of the "oppressed, down-trodden, and marginalized" of Pakistan. Bhatti said that he had dedicated his life to the "struggle for human equality, social justice, religious freedom, and to uplift and empower religious minority communities." He added that he wanted to send "a message of hope to the people living a life of disappointment, disillusionment, and despair." Pointedly, he also said that he would use his cabinet post to push for elimination of the blasphemy laws, which he flagged as a chief obstacle to the emancipation of religious minorities.

All that was combined with the fact that Bhatti believed Pakistan stood at a crossroads, as the situation for minorities on the ground, especially Christians, was becoming steadily worse. In an August 7, 2008, interview with *Avvenire*, the official newspaper of the Italian bishops' conference, he described the lay of the land as follows: "The situation is not at all positive, in fact it's getting worse. Christians suffer discrimination from a legislative point of view, churches are being burned, our women are violated and forcibly converted to Islam." As a result, he believed that only government intervention could turn things around, and he saw the post-Benazir Bhutto rule of the People's Party as an historic opportunity to effect change.

Bhatti's nomination was widely hailed by Pakistan's Christian leaders, especially within his own Catholic community. Peter Jacobs, at the time the secretary of the church's National Commission for Justice and Peace, described Bhatti as "the best choice for such a position" and said he was optimistic the new minister "will be able to play an important role in removing discriminatory legislation still existing in the country," especially "the widespread and improper use of the law on blasphemy," which Jacobs called "a major hindrance in interfaith harmony and dialogue."

In the end, the dream of a new Pakistan that drove Bhatti to his choice in 2008 turned out to be essentially hollow. Zardari's administration was marked by repeated charges of corruption and incompetence, and for presiding over increased terrorist violence in the country rather than curbing it. He ended with abysmally low approval ratings, sending the Pakistani People's Party to a crushing defeat in elections five years later. Nevertheless, with his characteristic "never look back" spirit, Bhatti threw himself into his new role with drive and verve, using his new platform to establish himself as a global point of reference in the press for religious freedom and minority rights.

Bhatti's Agenda

As a federal minister heading a department that employed roughly seventy-five people, Bhatti proved to be tireless in trying to promote minority rights in Pakistan, using his federal powers when he could and at least trying to point a direction when his position didn't afford him the direct authority to act.

One of Bhatti's first actions in his new post, just two weeks after he took the office, was to help broker a deal so that Sikhs could purchase land for the construction of a university, saying in a statement after he met with Sikh officials that it was a sign of the government's commitment "to protecting the rights of the religious minorities," describing it as part of a broader effort to transform Pakistan into "a modern, enlightened, and democratic state." In similar fashion, just days later Bhatti announced that security measures had been tightened at a Hindu temple in the Punjab region following a series of strikes in Mumbai, India, carried out by Islamic radicals that had left Hindus in Pakistan fearful for their safety. Bhatti even traveled to the Lord Shiva Temple at Katasraj in Punjab to host a dinner for pilgrims taking part in a Hindu festival in order to express his solidarity.

Shortly thereafter, Bhatti announced a new aid program for Sikh families affected by ongoing militancy in the country's northwest. During a visit to the area, Bhatti denounced moves by local Taliban forces to impose a tax on minority groups, insisting that minorities in Pakistan "are not conquered communities, rather they are sons of the soil and the government will not allow any faction of society to trample their constitutional rights."

It was not by accident that Bhatti's first high-profile actions as a government minister were intended to benefit Sikhs and Hindus, rather than Christians. At the beginning, there was a natural suspicion among other minority communities in Pakistan that because Bhatti was a Catholic, he might use his position largely to aid his fellow Christians rather than genuinely being concerned with the fate of all religious minorities in the country, and Bhatti was politically astute enough to realize that he needed to lay those concerns to rest right out of the gate if he was to be effective.

In early 2009 Bhatti helped to persuade the Zardari government to designate August 11 "Minority Day" in Pakistan, saying it would be a national observance "to honor the contribution and sacrifices of minorities in creation of Pakistan and nation-building." He cited a famous saying from Quaid-e-Azam Muhammad Ali Jinnah, Pakistan's founding father: "You are free; you are free to go to your temples, you are free to go to your mosques or to any other place of worship in this state of Pakistan. You may belong to any religion or caste or creed that has nothing to do with the business of the state."

Bhatti also helped spearhead what was styled as a major breakthrough for minorities in Pakistan in March 2009, when the government announced that 5 percent of all jobs in the federal government would be reserved for members of religious minorities. According to a notice issued by the federal employment division, the positions would be filled by direct recruitment and candidates would be selected on the basis of merit. Federal authorities also encouraged Pakistan's provincial governments to follow suit and set aside a share of positions for members of minority groups.

Official census figures peg minorities at around 3 percent of Pakistan's population, though leaders in minority communities have long insisted those numbers have been deliberately downplayed in order to minimize the minority footprint in the country. Employment quotas have been a long-standing demand of the country's minority groups, who routinely complain that they face chronic discrimination in hiring and in advancement once on the job.

At the same time as its reservation of federal jobs for religious minorities, the government also assured that four seats in the country's senate would be set aside for minority groups under the terms of the eighteenth amendment to the country's constitution. Bhatti also paved the way for decrees that members of religious minorities would be guaranteed paid vacation on the days of their major festivals, and that minority prisoners would benefit from a remission of their terms on the same days. On the prison front, Bhatti ensured that non-Muslim inmates in Pakistani jails would be assigned prayer rooms where prayer and worship services could be staged.

Capping what was arguably the most productive year of his term, Bhatti also launched a national campaign to promote interfaith harmony through seminars, awareness groups, and workshops; proposed that the national Ministry of Education introduce comparative religion courses as a compulsory curriculum subject, in order to foster awareness and appreciation of minority faiths; created a twenty-four-hour crisis hotline phone number to report acts of violence against minorities; and introduced a campaign to protect religious artifacts and sites that belong to minorities.

One of the first real crises Bhatti would face as minister came in early August 2009, when a series of riots broke out in Gojra, a town in Punjab, that resulted in the deaths of eight Christians, including a woman and four children. Islamic mobs in the area had been whipped into a frenzy by the rhetoric of radical groups describing Christians as "America's dogs," and the triggering incident was a rumor that Christians had desecrated pages from the Qur'an during a wedding ceremony. Forty Christian houses as well as a church were set ablaze, and the eight victims were burned alive. Eighteen other people were injured in the violence, and many Christians complained that police and security forces had stood by while the mobs carried out the assaults.

In response, Zardari directed Bhatti to head to Gojra and take personal responsibility for the government's response, ensuring people's safety and security. Bhatti would conclude that responsibility for the attacks belonged to a banned anti-Shi'ite militant group, and more than sixty-five people were arrested under the country's anti-terrorism laws. Even Pope Benedict XVI spoke out on the incident, calling it a "senseless attack" about which he was "deeply grieved" to hear.

Criticism from Outraged Christians

Despite Bhatti's efforts to address the Gojra crisis, he ran headlong into the outrage of the Christian community in the country, which saw the burning of a woman and children as the latest example of a system that simply didn't see their lives as valuable. The Pakistan Christian Congress, a group founded in 1985 to safeguard the rights of the country's Christians, publicly called on Bhatti and another government official to resign, arguing that neither the People's Party nor the other main political faction, the Pakistan Muslim League, was truly invested in Christian welfare, accusing Bhatti of acting as a "rubber stamp or tool of Muslim political groups." Among other things, the congress noted, past People's Party governments had nationalized Christian schools, colleges, and hospitals. The group also announced that instead of observing August 11 as Minority Day, it would mark it as "Black Day" to protest what it saw as hollow promises of appreciation and protection.

Bhatti eventually canceled the inaugural Minority Day celebrations, saying that in this context they would be inappropriate, but also perhaps fearing blowback from outraged Christians likely to interpret them as a government cover for inadequate efforts to provide security and legal accountability for violations of Christian rights.

When Zardari visited Italy in October 2009 and included Bhatti in his delegation during an encounter with Pope Benedict XVI, the *Pakistani Christian Post*, a media outlet that gives voice to the sentiments of aggrieved Christians in the country, was scathing in its editorial comment: "Shahbaz Bhatti has been selected by the present government to be a 'tool' to the Pakistani minorities and to appease the Western governments, when they object on Pakistan's subhuman treatment to its minorities," it wrote. "Bhatti is on the government's payroll, and in no way represents the minorities, since they never elected him. An average citizen does not even have access to this so-called representative of the minorities."

While in Rome for that October 2009 visit, Bhatti also arranged a meeting for Zardari with members of the Community of Sant'Egidio, one of the new movements in the Catholic Church. Sant'Egidio was founded in 1968 to serve the poor of Rome and has gone on to become a major player in both conflict resolution and also ecumenical and interfaith dialogue. Bhatti first got to know Sant'Egidio when they contributed to relief efforts for the 2005 Pakistan earthquake and remained close to the group throughout the remainder of his career. He visited the small Sant'Egidio community in Pakistan and also made several trips to the organization's headquarters in Rome's Trastevere neighborhood to discuss his work to promote interfaith understanding.

One possible sign of the imprint left on Bhatti by Sant'Egidio was his mounting focus on the abolition of the death penalty, which remained legal in Pakistan despite a moratorium on executions imposed in 2008. Sant'Egidio has been active in anti-death penalty efforts around the world, and, according to Rahael Gill, Bhatti's press secretary, at the time of his death Bhatti was planning on devoting special efforts to formally repealing capital punishment in Pakistan.

One key moment for Bhatti came around the same time as the meeting with the pope, when two suicide bombers launched simultaneous attacks on both the men's and the women's side of Islamabad's International Islamic University. Three female students were killed in the attack, but the death toll likely would have been much higher had it not been for the actions of a Christian janitor named Pervaiz Masih. He intercepted the bomber at the door of the girls' cafeteria and forced him to detonate outside, greatly reducing the students' exposure to the blast. Masih, who was killed, at the time had been on the job less than a week and was earning just sixty dollars a month.

Masih was immediately hailed as a hero, drawing wide praise from leading Muslim commentators. The university volunteered to give his three-year-old child a free education when it was time for her to attend university, and they also offered employment to his widow. The Pakistan government awarded the family compensation of $12,000 in recognition of Masih's bravery, and a professor at the university penned a tribute saying that Masih "rose above the barriers of caste, creed and sectarian terrorism. Despite being a Christian, he sacrificed his life to save the Muslim girls."

Bhatti joined the chorus of praise, saying, "He is a national hero because he saved the life of many girls. As a Christian, a person of minority, he stood in front of the Taliban to protect the university." For the rest of his term, Bhatti would often point to Masih as an example of the true role of religious minorities in Pakistan and an example of why the state had to do a better job of assuring those minorities that they too have a place in the nation.

As the calendar turned to 2010, Bhatti decided to return to what had long been a personal crusade, now backed by the power of his federal position: sweeping change to Pakistan's blasphemy laws, which minorities in the country generally see as the single greatest threat to their security and peace of mind, given the long-standing pattern of abuse of those laws to settle personal scores or to lash out against perceived enemies. In an interview with Agence France-Presse (AFP) in February, Bhatti announced that the government's aim was to overhaul the blasphemy laws by the end of the year.

"We are striving for human equality, religious freedom, social justice, interfaith harmony and equal rights for minorities in Pakistan. . . . These discriminatory laws are against the vision of the founding father and the spirit of democracy," he said. "We are making such changes and amendments in these laws so that they cannot be misused and used to create insecurity among minorities. We are in the process of consultation, and after consulting with all the stakeholders—political parties, Islamic religious scholars, Ulema and representatives of minorities—[and then] we will table a bill in parliament."

"It is part of my mission to serve the marginalized and down-trodden minorities of Pakistan," he said in July 2010. "I have a commitment to serve the oppressed people of Pakistan till my last breath."

Bhatti faced criticism for pursuing only a reform of the blasphemy laws rather than a complete repeal, but in various interviews he appeared to suggest that the right kind of reform would solve the problem. Skeptics, however, expressed doubt that any changes would go beyond the cosmetic, since the People's Party, despite its secular platform, still relied on support from various Islamic groupings in order to maintain its majority in Pakistan's parliament. Bhatti, however, insisted he was pressing for real reform, including inserting strong penalties into the statute for making false allegations and also shifting responsibility for investigation and enforcement away from local police, who were frequently accused of being aligned with extremist groups, toward district or regional officials.

"We are well aware of the misuse of the blasphemy law," Bhatti said. "Many innocent people of Pakistan, belonging to both Muslim and non-Muslim communities, are falsely implicated under the pretext of the blasphemy law. Mostly this law is used to settle personal scores, and no one commits blasphemy due to political or religious enmity. It is important to promote tolerance in our society, so that people of different faiths can live in unity and harmony." For his trouble, several Islamic religious parties in Pakistan demanded Bhatti's removal as a minister in November 2010, citing his outspoken opposition to the blasphemy laws.

Bhatti experienced what he would describe to family and friends as one of the real highlights of his career in September 2010 when he again traveled to Rome, this time to be received by Pope Benedict XVI in a private audience at the pontiff's summer residence of Castel Gandolfo. The meeting came shortly after a series of floods had struck several regions of Pakistan, affecting an estimated 20 million people and one-fifth of the country's landmass, and leaving more than 2,000 people dead.

In the session, Benedict told Bhatti that "the flood affected persons who were very close to my heart, and we stand in solidarity with Pakistan. We will continue to support the victims of this devastation, for which I have made appeals." For his part, Bhatti expressed gratitude for the way Catholic relief agencies in various parts of the world had come to the country's aid, saying, "Pakistan needed the support and cooperation of the international community to deal with a natural disaster of this scale and magnitude." Bhatti also presented a letter to Benedict from Zardari pledging Pakistan's commitment to interfaith and intercultural harmony.

The Asia Bibi Firestorm

The greatest firestorm Bhatti would confront during his brief, twenty-eight-month run as a federal minister broke out in November 2010, when a Punjabi judge sentenced a

Christian woman named Asia Bibi to death under the very blasphemy laws Bhatti had pledged essentially to abrogate. As mentioned in chapter three, Bibi is a Catholic and a mother of five; she was an illiterate agricultural worker at the time of her arrest. It was the first time a woman was sentenced to death for the crime of blasphemy, and just a few months before a Muslim couple had been assigned life imprisonment for essentially the same crime.

Bibi later reconstructed what happened. She had been harvesting berries with a group of Muslim women in June 2009 when a dispute broke out after she drank water from the same well as the Muslim women. Words were exchanged, and later some of the Muslim women accused Bibi of having insulted the Prophet Muhammad. She was arrested and imprisoned, but had a lesser punishment been imposed it's unlikely her case would have attracted broad national and international interest. Because she was sentenced to death, however, her situation trained a global spotlight on Pakistan and its blasphemy laws and put Bibi's fellow Catholic and minister of minorities affairs squarely in the middle of the drama. Various global figures called for Bibi's release, including Pope Benedict XVI, and protest rallies and marches were organized up and down Pakistan. In late November 2010, French Cardinal Jean-Louis Tauran, president of the Vatican's Pontifical Council for Interreligious Dialogue, used a preplanned trip to Pakistan, including a meeting with Zardari and Bhatti, to press for clemency for Bibi.

Bhatti was tasked by the federal government with establishing the details of the case and swiftly declared that he believed Bibi to be innocent. In his report Bhatti concluded that the case against Bibi had been "built by Muslim fundamentalists merely upon the commonplace hatred harbored against Christians, disdainfully referring to them as 'untouchables' or *Choohra* and *Bhangi*," derogatory words frequently used to denigrate Christians in the Punjabi or Sindhi languages, respectively. He asserted that on-the-ground witnesses "unanimously declared her innocent," and recommended that she be pardoned should her legal appeals be denied or unduly delayed. The governor of Punjab at the time, Salmaan Taseer, joined Bhatti's call for a pardon for Bibi, foreshadowing the fate both men would suffer for their outspokenness on the Bibi case and in opposition to the blasphemy laws. Even before the Bibi case erupted, Bhatti had told reporters that he had received death threats for his stance, including one threat that he would be beheaded should he continue.

For his part, Taseer predicted Zadari would do the right thing. "He's a liberal, modern-minded president, and he's not going to see a poor woman like this targeted and executed. . . . It's just not going to happen," he said. "The blasphemy law is not a God-made law. It's a man-made law. . . . It's a law that gives an excuse to extremists and reactionaries to target weak people and minorities."

The call to pardon Bibi was hardly universal. At the same time Bhatti was delivering his report insisting on her innocence, two prominent Muslim clerics warned Zadari against any move to show clemency. "If the president pardons Asia Bibi, we will raise our voices across the country until he is forced to take his decision back," said a nationally known mufti named Muneer Ur Rehman. Hafiz Ibtisam Elahi Zaheer, a leading cleric in Lahore, said pardoning the woman would be "criminal negligence" and would cause enhanced interreligious tension. Bhatti also appeared on a national news program called *News Beat* on November 30, where the other guests were clearly in support of the blasphemy law and the tone of the questions directed to Bhatti by host Behar Mukhari was largely hostile.

Undeterred, Bhatti arranged for Bibi's daughters to visit his Islamabad office. He told reporters that he would press Zardari to intervene in the case if the legal process became bogged down in delays or procedural disputes. He also used the occasion of the sentence to renew his press for a sweeping overhaul of the blasphemy laws, calling them "a tool in the hands of the extremists." He told the Catholic news outlet Asia News, "The blasphemy law is often used as a tool to settle personal differences, and 85 percent of such cases are false cases."

"I will go to every knock for justice on her [Bibi's] behalf, and I will take all steps for her protection," Bhatti vowed, and in the meantime he sent a letter to the inspector general of the country's penal system, demanding that Bibi's safety be assured while behind bars.

Responding to fears that Bibi might be freed, a hardline Muslim cleric issued a fatwa and put a price on her head, pledging to pay the equivalent of $10,000 to anyone who killed her—a princely sum by the standards of the country's poor. Bhatti condemned the announcement as "immoral, unjust, and irresponsible," and promised that "every legal and constitutional means will be adopted" in her case.

Despite Bhatti's best efforts, by the end of 2010 it began to seem that he was losing the internal battle within the Zadari government to free Bibi and to revise the blasphemy law. When a former minister and People's Party member named Sherry Rehman introduced a bill based on Bhatti's own suggestions about changes to the law, a government spokesman essentially disowned Bhatti and promised that Zadari would not seek revisions. "We [the government] have no intention of repealing the blasphemy law . . . ensuring the respect of the Holy Prophet Muhammad is part of our faith," said religious affairs minister Khursheed Shah in a

December 30 statement. Many observers concluded that Islamic groupings in parliament had threatened to bring down the Zadari government had it moved forward.

That's where things stood as 2011 began, and Bhatti would not have to wait long for the next thunderclap in the Bibi saga.

On January 4, 2011, Taseer, a Muslim and the governor of Punjab who had joined Bhatti in calling for Bibi's release, was shot dead by his own bodyguard in Islamabad's Kohsar Market, a spot often frequented by foreigners in the capital city. The bodyguard, Malik Mumtaz Hussain Qadri, was arrested and confessed to assassinating Taseer because "he did blasphemy of the Prophet Mohammed," according to a police spokesman. Taseer was transported to a hospital after the shooting but was dead upon arrival, the spokesman said. Doctors would later account for an astonishing total of twenty-six gunshots in Taseer's chest, face, neck, and legs, with some of the bullets having passed cleanly through his body.

Bhatti's reaction to the assassination was swift and unequivocal.

"I will continue," Bhatti told CNN. "I will campaign for this . . . these fanatics cannot stop me from moving any further steps against the misuse of (the) blasphemy law." He said he was not in fear for his life but conceded, "I am getting threats. I was told by the religious extremists that if you will make any amendments in this law, you will be killed. But I am ready to sacrifice my life for the principled stand I have taken because the people of Pakistan are being victimized under the pretense of blasphemy law."

Despite international revulsion over Taseer's murder, conservative Islamist groups maintained their pressure in defense of the blasphemy laws and the Bibi prosecution. On January 9, an estimated 50,000 people marched through the streets of Karachi, Pakistan's largest city, in defense of the law. In chilling rhetoric, Fazlur Rehman, head of the Taliban-linked conservative religious party Jamiat Ulema Islam, told the cheering crowd that if "the rulers are out to defend Taseer, so we also have the right to legally defend Mumtaz Qadri," referring to Taseer's assassin, and added that Taseer "was responsible for his own murder" because he had criticized the law. The crowd responded with chants of "Courage and bravery, Qadri, Qadri." Many wore headbands and armbands inscribed, "We are ready to sacrifice our lives for the sanctity of the prophet."

On January 29, a similar rally took place, again in Karachi, but this time led by the women's wing of the Islamic movement, Jamaat-e-Islami. Addressing the crowd, Islamic leader Ghafoor Ahmed thundered that "no attempt to touch the law will be allowed" and promised that the country "will soon become a true Islamic nation." Once again speakers heaped praise on Taseer's killer, with one rally organizer hailing him as "a hero of the Muslim ummah." Members of the fundamentalist movement also demanded the expulsion of all Vatican officials in Pakistan, for what they called "interference" in internal affairs by Pope Benedict XVI for calling for the country's blasphemy laws to be abrogated in a speech to diplomats earlier in the month.

Further illustrating the national ferment the Bibi case generated, the next day rival rallies were held—one by Islamic fundamentalists in support of the blasphemy laws, with speakers vowing a "long march" to Islamabad should Asia Bibi be freed, essentially code for a threat to overthrow the government, and another called by Bishop Anthony Rufin of Islamabad-Rawalpindi in support of Bibi and in favor of peace and interfaith harmony across Pakistan. During a rally staged by Islamic fundamentalists in Lahore, Pope

Benedict, Bhatti, and the Christian cross were all burned in effigy, in front of a crowd of more than 40,000 cheering demonstrators.

Ever defiant, Bhatti vowed that the fundamentalist demonstrations would not deter the government from amending the blasphemy laws, which he said were being abused by Muslim extremists to victimize minorities. He warned that religious leaders who preach violence could be charged with inciting murder if the debate claims another life. "We will not be intimidated," Bhatti said. "We cannot remain silent on the victimization and growing extremism."

By early 2011 it was clear that Bhatti was in the crosshairs of angry radicals who saw him as the leader of the press to free Bibi, to roll back the blasphemy laws, and to secularize the country. Archbishop Lawrence Saldhana of Lahore acknowledged the realities of the situation, saying, "Minister Bhatti is experiencing a very difficult time, targeted by extremists. On behalf of all Christians in Pakistan, we wish to express to the minister our complete solidarity and gratitude for his social and political commitment to defending religious minorities."

That solidarity, however, did little to advance Bhatti's agenda. In early February, Rehman, the member of parliament who had introduced legislation to amend the blasphemy law in keeping with Bhatti's vision, announced her bill was dead because the Zadari government wasn't behind it. At the time she was largely confined to her home under a sort of voluntary house arrest because of death threats and blamed her own People's Party government for caving into extremists. "The procedural amendments I sought would have given relief to innocent people, that's all," said Rehman, a former information minister. "Instead it has become the object of a power play between parties."

This was the landscape in Pakistan as February 2011 gave way to March: Bhatti's vision of a pluralistic, secular society in which minorities would be full players in national life seemed to be slipping away; his drive to amend the blasphemy laws that had been the central objective of his political career had stalled; Asia Bibi remained in prison; and Bhatti's own life was under threat. As a few days would prove, those threats were hardly idle.

CHAPTER FIVE

Death Comes for the Minister

March 2, 2011, was an overcast Wednesday in Islamabad. Shahbaz Bhatti was leaving the home he shared with his mother in a residential neighborhood; she had moved to the national capital after the death of her husband, Jacob, in order to be close to her youngest son. Bhatti, the country's minister for minorities affairs, was running late for a cabinet meeting. Despite the multiple death threats he had received, he was traveling without the security escort vehicle that's standard practice for federal ministers in the country. This would be one of several elements related to Bhatti's death that would later generate controversy and conspiracy theories.

A small, white Suzuki was blocking the way as Bhatti's driver, Gul Sher, attempted to pull his black Toyota Corolla out from the area, making it clear that the assassins had been staking out Bhatti's home, waiting for him to exit. Before Sher could move the car more than a yard, two armed men, wearing the traditional Pakistani garb of baggy pants and long tunics, jumped out of the Suzuki and opened fire with automatic weapons. After an initial burst, one man dragged Sher from the vehicle and the other continued firing continuous bursts through a side window. In the end Bhatti was struck at least eight times, leaving him dead on the scene. Police eventually recovered twenty-five shell casings from two Kalishikov automatic rifles at the crime scene.

An autopsy would show that the cause of death was from multiple bullets that had struck Bhatti in the skull, rupturing it. Bhatti's upper torso was "riddled with bullets. His skull, heart, lungs, and other vital organs were all ruptured. However, there were no wounds on his limbs," said an official in the Pakistan Institute of Medical Sciences where the post-mortem examination was conducted. Bhatti was forty-two at the time of his death.

Before calmly leaving the scene, the gunmen dropped leaflets around the car that described Bhatti as a "Christian infidel" and "blasphemer," which were signed "Taliban al-Qaida Punjab," meaning Bhatti's home region of Pakistan. Observers noted that in an additional sign of brazenness, the gunmen didn't attempt to eliminate any forensic evidence before they fled, nor did they execute the main witness, Sher, who suffered only minor injuries.

"With the blessing of Allah, the *mujahideen* will send each of you to hell," said the note, a clear threat to anyone who would agree to serve on a committee to revise Pakistan's blasphemy laws that Bhatti had vowed to form. "This is a lesson to the world of infidel crusaders and Jews, and their allies in the Muslim world," the pamphlet said, warning that "either you or us will live in this world."

According to a doctor who lived in the area and witnessed the shooting, it took Islamabad police a full fifteen minutes to arrive on the scene after the gunmen had driven away. When the police did eventually come, Bhatti was transferred to the nearby Shifa Hospital and was pronounced dead upon arrival.

"It lasted about twenty seconds," said a neighbor, Naseem Javed. "When I rushed out I saw the minister's driver standing by the car, shivering, and his [Bhatti's] niece weeping and shouting."

That niece was twenty-two-year-old Mariam Bhatti, who was staying in the house with her uncle and his mother, and who had immediately run outside upon hearing the gunfire.

"I rushed out to find his body covered with blood. I said 'uncle, uncle' and tried to take his pulse. But he was already dead," she would tell a reporter later that day, extending her palm to show Bhatti's blood that she had not yet had the heart to wash away.

Tehrik-i-Taliban, a Pakistan-based offshoot of the Taliban, told the BBC that Bhatti's murder was intended to send a message.

"This man was a known blasphemer of the Prophet [Muhammad]," said the group's deputy spokesman, Ahsanullah Ahsan. "We will continue to target all those who speak against the law which punishes those who insult the prophet. Their fate will be the same."

Illustrating the deep climate of fear the twin murders of Salmaan Taseer, the Punjabi governor, and Bhatti had generated in Pakistan, President Asif Ali Zardari didn't even attend Bhatti's funeral, citing concern for his personal safety. Neither did most of the supporters of Bhatti's campaign to eliminate the blasphemy laws, including parliamentarian Sherry Rehman, who by that stage was in hiding and later would be named ambassador to the United States.

In the immediate wake of the assassination, the question of why Bhatti had not been protected by security personnel loomed large in public reaction, especially given the murder of Taseer and the multiple public occasions in which Bhatti had acknowledged having received explicit threats to his life.

Initially a police spokesman said that Bhatti did indeed have a security escort but had left it at home—an almost laughable assertion, given that the assault unfolded just over one yard from Bhatti's residence, which would have afforded the phantom escort plenty of time to react had it actually been present.

Later the Islamabad police headquarters issued a statement saying that Bhatti had relieved his security escort on Tuesday at 11:00 p.m., telling them he would join up with them again Wednesday morning when he arrived at work. The statement also claimed that fifteen security personnel, including police commandos and Pakistan's Frontier Constabulary personnel, had been deployed for providing security to Bhatti but said they had been confined to his office at the minister's personal request.

However, one police source said at the time it shouldn't have mattered what Bhatti wanted, since standard operating procedure for security escorts for VIPs such as federal ministers was to remain with the subject they're guarding at all times, regardless of their personal desires. Further, the claim that Bhatti had shrugged off his protection clashed with accounts from figures such as Jason Kenny, at the time Canada's citizenship and immigration minister, who recounted that, on a visit to Canada shortly before his death, Bhatti told Kenny he felt he wasn't being adequately protected and even asked the Canadian government to lobby the Pakistani authorities on his behalf.

As time went on, the apparent lapse in security procedures would fuel conspiracy theories among some aggrieved members of minority groups, especially Christians, as well as some human rights activists, who wondered if elements in the security services sympathetic to Islamic radical groups had arranged for a gap in Bhatti's protection to allow the assassination to be carried out.

Another front of controversy opened up in the immediate wake of the attack, when some Islamabad police sources initially suggested the trappings of Islamic radicalism left at the scene may have been a ruse, and perhaps the real motive for the murder was linked to internal tensions among Christian groups, noting that Bhatti over the years had drawn strong criticism from some of his fellow Christians. Some Pakistani newspapers reported anonymous police sources were looking at the possibility there were tensions within the Bhatti family itself, linked to a property dispute. Those suggestions infuriated Bhatti's family and supporters, as did the fact that an initial probe of the murder seemed to go nowhere. In late June 2011 the chief of a joint investigation team, Tahir Alam, announced that in his view the file should be closed for "lack of evidence." After interrogating 519 suspects, including Mumtaz Qadri, who had killed Punjab Governor Salmaan Taseer, Alam said that the joint team had nothing to go on to find the culprits.

Adding to the atmosphere of suspicion among Pakistan's Christian community was the fact that while Bhatti was clearly the highest-profile Christian killed with apparent impunity around that time, he was hardly the only one. On June 21, for instance, a Christian street cleaner in Lahore named Abas Masih was stabbed to death by a Muslim merchant after he refused to immediately clear the area in front of the merchant's shop. Police initially declined to press charges, and only after wide coverage of the incident reluctantly made an arrest.

Two years after Bhatti's murder, two suspects were arrested and charged with the crime. One was eventually acquitted for lack of evidence, and another was released on roughly $10,000 bail a year later, citing medical grounds, despite the fact he actually confessed killing Bhatti to the police. Sikander Bhatti, one of Shahbaz's brothers, said at the time, "If one of the men accused of killing my brother has been released on bail, then how to expect justice in the case? The problem is that even judges are afraid of the terrorists."

That fear is not unreasonable, given that a chief prosecutor in the Bhatti case, Chaudhry Zulfiqar, was shot dead in broad daylight in Islamabad in May 2013. As with Bhatti, gunmen emerged from a car and riddled Zulfiqar's vehicle with bullets, leaving him dead on the scene. One of the gunmen who shot Zulfiqar, Umer Abdullah, was injured when the prosecutor's driver returned fire and was taken into custody where he confessed to also having been involved in the assassination of Bhatti.

The terror such acts generate is palpable. Shortly after Zulfiqar's assassination, a judge from the Islamabad high court recused himself from hearing the case against one of Bhatti's alleged assassins, citing a "conflict of interest" since the accused was the son of a retired lieutenant colonel in the Pakistani army in which the judge had also served. It was becoming difficult to find either prosecutors or judges willing to carry the case forward.

Finding witnesses willing to testify also became an equally vexing challenge. Even Bhatti's oldest brother Paul, who had returned to Pakistan from Italy to carry on his brother's work, left the country ahead of a scheduled court hearing after the Tehrik-i-Taliban dropped a threatening letter at his Faisalabad office. In late December 2016 an antiterrorism military court to which jurisdiction for the prosecution had been transferred announced yet another delay after seven witnesses in the case did not appear for a scheduled hearing.

By that stage two other Islamic radicals had also been charged in Bhatti's death after being arrested for an attack on a mosque, but many experts doubt any of the remaining accused will ever see the inside of a prison cell. Whatever the future may bring, more than five years after Bhatti was shot to death, not a single person has ever been convicted or sentenced for the crime.

Foreshadowing

Though the brutal killing on March 2 generated shock around the world, perhaps the person least likely to be surprised that morning may have been the victim himself. For years Bhatti had lived with the awareness that his campaigns for minority rights and against the blasphemy laws would trigger powerful, and sometimes violent, opposition, and he always knew assassination was a possible outcome. As far back as 2005 while he was still running the All-Pakistan Minorities Alliance, Bhatti had said, "I want to live for Christ, and I want to die for him."

Shortly after the January murder of Taseer, Bhatti had told the AFP news agency that he understood he was now public enemy number one for the country's radical forces and expressed skepticism that enhanced security would be of much help.

"I'm not talking about special security arrangements," he said. "We need to stand against these forces of terrorism because they're terrorizing the country. I cannot trust in security. . . . I believe that protection can come only from heaven, so these bodyguards can't save you."

In an interview with the Pakistani newspaper *The Express Tribune* and a correspondent from a German newspaper two days before his death, Bhatti seemed to have a clear sense of what lay ahead.

"I know I am target number one for them (extremists) now after they succeeded in eliminating Salmaan Taseer," he said. "And frankly, let me tell you, I think they will get me one day." Defiantly, however, he added, "I won't change my thinking towards a certain issue on the dictates of someone. I'll continue to pursue my ideals for Pakistan; my dreams for the country."

Kenny, the Canadian minister, said much the same thing. As Bhatti was leaving the country, Kenny said Bhatti told him, "I have no choice but to go back and support my brothers and sisters. When they kill me, please do what you can to take care of my family." That comment, Kenny said, came three weeks before March 2, 2011.

"I had this truly eerie feeling being around him of being in the presence of someone under the shadow of death," Kenny said. "There was no doubt in his mind that he was going back to face potentially lethal violence. It was only for him a matter of when, and not if."

During that same Canadian visit, Bhatti gave an interview to the Catholic News Service, in which he openly acknowledged the risks he was running.

"I have been told by pro-Taliban religious extremists that if I continue to speak against the blasphemy law, I will be beheaded," he said. "As a Christian, I believe Jesus is my strength. He has given me a power and wisdom and motivation to serve suffering humanity. I follow the principles of my conscience, and I am ready to die and sacrifice my life for the principles I believe."

All that's in keeping with a striking aspect of any number of martyrologies, which is how the person heading for death seems to have a premonition of what's coming. For instance Archbishop Oscar Romero told a Mexican newspaper in his final interview, just two weeks before he was shot to death while saying Mass in 1980, "If am killed, I shall rise again in the Salvadoran people."

So too with Shahbaz Bhatti, who recorded a video message four months before his own assassination, which he requested be released in the event of his death. The video was recorded in the context of a December 2010 interview with Johan Candelin, a goodwill ambassador for the freedom of expression group First Step Forum, an outgrowth of the World Evangelical Alliance, which also promotes ecumenical and interfaith dialogue.

"It's sort of his testimony to the world," Candelin said, who worked with Bhatti for about seven years and interviewed him several times. He said that Bhatti had "very much come to terms with the prospect of his own murder," saying, "I know that the leader of the Taliban called him directly on his mobile phone and said, 'We will kill you unless you stop.' They also called his father a month ago."

Here's the full text of that video message, which can easily still be found online. Bhatti spoke in response to a question about the sorts of threats to his life he was facing due to his political activity.

> The forces of violence, banned military organizations, the Taliban, and Al-Qaeda. They want to impose their radical philosophy in Pakistan. Whoever stands against their radical philosophy, they threaten them. When I'm leading this campaign against the sharia laws, for the abolishment of the blasphemy law, and speaking for the persecuted, oppressed and marginalized Christians, and other minorities, these Taliban threaten me. But I want to share that I believe in Jesus Christ, who has given his own life for us. I know what is the meaning of the Cross, and I'm following the Cross. I'm ready to die for a cause, I'm living for my community and suffering people, and I will die to defend their rights. These threats and these warnings cannot change my opinion and principles. I prefer to die for my

principles and for justice for my community rather than to compromise [because of] these threats.

Reaction

A funeral Mass for the slain minister took place on March 4, 2011, just two days after the assassination. It was held in Khushpur, Bhatti's native village in Punjab and arguably the country's Catholic stronghold, meaning that, in the end, Bhatti returned to where it all began. An estimated 20,000 people packed the streets of Khushpur to pay tribute to Bhatti, most of them drawn from his own Christian community. His casket was draped both by the flag of Pakistan and the banner of the All-Pakistan Minorities Alliance, the group he had founded and that in many ways represented his legacy. The funeral Mass was led by Bishop Joseph Coutts of Faisalabad and was attended by two Protestant bishops and dozens of Catholic priests.

Peter Jacob, executive secretary of the Pakistani bishops' justice and peace commission, told the Catholic News Service by phone from Khushpur, "It was a very emotional funeral, with the people wailing and weeping all through."

"The killers have snatched our hero," said Bhatti's brother Sikander during the funeral, which was surrounded by a thick security cordon. After the service, Bhatti's body was buried in the Khushpur cemetery alongside other members of his family.

Earlier in the day, a separate funeral was held in Fatima Church in Islamabad, the national capital, in order to accommodate government officials and other VIPs who either couldn't or didn't want to make the trip to Khushpur, in part perhaps out of security concerns. It was led by Bishop Rufin Anthony of Islamabad-Rawalpindi.

Pakistan's then-prime minister Yousuf Raza Gilani delivered a paean to Bhatti before the packed congregation, saying, "People like him, they are very rare. All the minorities have lost a great leader. I assure you, we will try our utmost to bring the culprits to justice." Gilani also announced an official three-day mourning period, ordering flags to be flown at half-mast, and saying, "Anti-state elements are making their last-ditch efforts by targeting important personalities in the country in order to fulfill their evil designs."

In the immediate wake of Bhatti's death, expressions of both outrage over the murder and appreciation for Bhatti's legacy flowed in from around the world. One of the first global figures to speak out was Pope Benedict XVI, who by that stage had met Bhatti twice and knew his work well. Benedict's spokesman at the time, Jesuit Fr. Federico Lombardi, issued the following statement as soon as news reached the Vatican on March 2.

> The assassination of Pakistan's Minister for Minorities, Shahbaz Bhatti, is a new and terrible grave act of violence. It demonstrates how correct the insistent calls of the Pope are with regard to violence against Christians and against religious liberty in general. Bhatti was the first Catholic to hold such a role. We remember that he was received by the Holy Father last September, and gave witness to his commitment to the peaceful coexistence among the religious communities of his nation. To prayers for the victim, condemnation of this senseless act of violence, and closeness to the Christians of Pakistan who are struck by hatred, is added an appeal to all to realize the dramatic urgency of the defense of religious liberty and of Christians who are the targets of violence and persecution.

A few days later, speaking during his traditional Sunday Angelus address, the pontiff returned to Bhatti, saying, "I ask the Lord Jesus that the moving sacrifice of the life of the Pakistani minister Shahbaz Bhatti may arouse in people's consciences the courage and commitment to defend the religious freedom of all men and, in this way, to promote their equal dignity."

Also on March 2, US president Barack Obama offered his own tribute, released by the White House Press Office.

> I am deeply saddened by the assassination of Pakistan's Minister for Minority Affairs Shahbaz Bhatti today in Islamabad, and condemn in the strongest possible terms this horrific act of violence. We offer our profound condolences to his family, loved ones and all who knew and worked with him. Minister Bhatti fought for and sacrificed his life for the universal values that Pakistanis, Americans and people around the world hold dear—the right to speak one's mind, to practice one's religion as one chooses, and to be free from discrimination based on one's background or beliefs. He was clear-eyed about the risks of speaking out, and, despite innumerable death threats, he insisted he had a duty to his fellow Pakistanis to defend equal rights and tolerance from those who preach division, hate, and violence. He most courageously challenged the blasphemy laws of Pakistan under which individuals have been prosecuted for speaking their minds or practicing their own faiths. Those who committed this crime should be brought to justice, and those who share Mr. Bhatti's vision of tolerance and religious freedom must be able to live free from fear. Minister Bhatti will be missed by all who knew him, and the United States will continue to stand with those who are dedicated to his vision of tolerance and dignity for all human beings.

Then-Secretary of State Hillary Clinton also released a statement about Bhatti's death.

I recently had the opportunity to meet with Minister Bhatti. He was a very impressive, courageous man. He was a patriot. He was a man of great conviction. He cared deeply for Pakistan and he had dedicated his life to helping the least among us. When I spoke with him, he was well aware of the drumbeat of threats against him. Despite those threats, when the Pakistan Government was recently reshuffled and the cabinet shrunk, he agreed to continue his work as the Minister for Minorities. And on behalf of the United States, I extend our deepest condolences to his family, his friends, and his colleagues.

Tributes, however, didn't just come from Western leaders or from Bhatti's fellow Christians inside Pakistan. Many like-minded members of other religious communities in the country also honored Bhatti's memory, including several Muslims who shared his vision of a pluralistic society in which minorities would be guaranteed a place at the table.

Imam Inayat Ali Shakir, for instance, said that Bhatti was not a "leader and hero of Christians alone; he fought for all religious minorities of Pakistan." Therefore, Shakir said, "His assassination is mourned by people of Pakistan and all those who are struggling for rights. He further said, "The killing of Shahbaz Bhatti is the killing of interfaith harmony and of peace."

Maulana Mehfooz Khan, an imam in Lahore and a member of the Islamic Ideology Council, is one of those struggling for respect of minority rights. Over the years, he developed a close relationship with the slain minister, based on friendship and respect. He called Bhatti "an ambassador of interfaith harmony. His services for the minorities of Pakistan are highly appreciated. He stood firm for what he believed in," and vowed that "his sacrifice will not go in vain, he will be remembered as a voice for the voiceless."

Iftikhar Ahmad, district coordinator of SPARK (a Muslim children's rights committee) in Faisalabad said, "I worked a lot with Shahbaz Bhatti against the blasphemy laws, Hudood Ordinance, and the Sharia Bill. The minister's assassination was clearly connected with extremism, and I am pained. . . . Unfortunately, our state is not taking adequate steps against the extremism that caused the brutal assassination and extra-judicial killing of Shahbaz Bhatti and Salmaan Taseer. I salute Shahbaz Bhatti's tireless and courageous efforts. He was not only a leader of minorities, but a true human rights defender too."

Pakistani poet Syed Najeeb Ali Shah lauded Bhatti, saying he was speaking on behalf of his fellow "poets, writers, and educators" for Bhatti's "struggle in favor of democracy and secularism."

Inevitably much of the most fulsome praise for the slain Bhatti came from his fellow Catholics, including bishops whom Bhatti had known personally and with whom he had worked over the years.

Bishop Rufin Anthony of Islamabad-Rawalpindi, for instance, was born in Khushpur like Bhatti, had come to know him well, and said his death represents the "tragic loss of a brave and faithful man."

"I knew him since the 1980s as he went to a school in Khushpur, his village in Faisalabad District," Rufin said. "He was always ready to work for the nation. Together, we founded Christian Liberation Front. He had a passion for minorities and fought for their rights. I met him a couple of weeks before his assassination. He surely saw it coming; yet, he was steadfast—such an inspiration to all who profess the Christian faith."

Archbishop Lawrence Saldanha of Lahore, who would retire just a month after Bhatti's death and who now lives in Toronto, was equally forceful in his assessment of Bhatti's legacy.

> Shahbaz Bhatti left a deep impression of an honest and deeply committed public servant. He was quite different from the rest of the self-serving and corrupt politicians. He was a staunch, practicing Catholic and inspired by the life of Jesus Christ. Like Christ, he stood up for truth, justice and freedom for the common man. He was honest in awarding construction contracts, unlike the usual politician who generally takes his commission. This witness of imitation of Christ finally led him to shed his blood for his people. He is considered a martyr by the Christian people, and they mourn the loss of a committed champion of their rights.

His longtime friend and mentor Cecil Chaudhry, who died in 2012, also tried to crystalize Bhatti's legacy.

> He was one of the most committed persons that I've ever come across. He committed himself to his cause at the age of 18 and he stuck to it. He realized that the only solution to the problem of the country is for the country to be what the father of the nation had envisioned it to be: a secular state where everybody has a right to live, where every single human being has equal rights with the other. That was his conviction, and that was his mission. To make Pakistan into Jinnah's Pakistan.

Two years after Bhatti's assassination, his oldest brother Paul was in Rome at the invitation of the Community of Sant'Egidio, the movement Shahbaz Bhatti had befriended at the time of the 2005 Kashmir earthquake and with which he had a strong bond over the years. Since his brother's death, Paul Bhatti had founded both the Shahbaz Bhatti Memorial Trust in Pakistan, to preserve his brother's legacy, and the Missione Shahbaz Bhatti Onlus, a companion foundation in Italy, where Paul Bhatti lived and worked as a surgeon.

At that time Pope Francis had convened a meeting of new movements on the feast of Pentecost in St. Peter's Square, and Paul Bhatti was given the opportunity to summarize his brother's legacy for the pope on behalf of Sant'Egidio. Here are some excerpts from what Paul Bhatti told the pope that day.

> In my country, Christians are a small minority, very poor. Faith in Jesus, the love of the gospel and unity with our mother the Church, are our only wealth. We suffer discrimination, and even violence. . . . But as disciples of Jesus, we want to be men of peace, in dialogue with our Muslim brothers and other religions. We want to bear witness to the love and mercy of our faith in Jesus.
>
> This was the testimony of my younger brother, Shahbaz Bhatti, who gave his life for the Gospel. Shahbaz began his mission among the poor and marginalized while attending school in our village, Khushpur. One Good Friday, in front of the cross of Jesus, he felt called—these are his words—to "match [God's] love by giving love to our brothers and sisters, placing myself at the service of Christians, especially the poor, the needy and the persecuted living in this country."
>
> Throughout his life, despite adversity and threats, he was faithful to that mission of being close to the poor, to witness the love of Jesus, working to ensure that the divided and violent society of Pakistan find the love and the ability to live together. The needy, the poor, the orphans, he said, "are the persecuted and needy part of the body of Christ."
>
> He dreamed of a peaceful Pakistan without discrimination, where believers of all faiths could enjoy equal rights, religious freedom and equal opportunity for the advancement of the country.

When he became Federal Minister for Minorities Affairs, he worked [to promote] harmony, tolerance and equality in a free society. He never ceased to be with the poor. When Pakistan was hit by floods and earthquakes, Shahbaz was there, close to those who suffered.

We asked him to be cautious, because his life was in grave danger, but he smiled, saying: "I put myself in the hands of Jesus and he will protect me." His faith was nourished by prayer and constant reading of the Gospel. Every morning, before he left home, Shahbaz remained alone in prayer, at least half an hour, with his Bible. Today the Bible, a true relic is kept here in Rome, in the Basilica of St. Bartholomew, the memorial of the new martyrs of our time, entrusted to my friends of the Community of Sant'Egidio, for which I am grateful. Christians in Pakistan are happy that his Bible is here in Rome, next to the memory of so many new martyrs and the apostles Peter and Paul.

Shahbaz Bhatti has borne witness to Jesus Christ with his blood. His life and his faith have borne fruit. I saw him, after his death, how many people loved him: the Christians, who had found in him a protection, a strong voice. But also many Muslims—ordinary people, scholars, imams of mosques—Hindus and Sikhs, crying and talking about him, saying that he was a man of peace, a man of God His great faith has exceeded the mountains of division so high in my country. It has sown a love higher than these mountains.

His words and his gestures gave courage to the Pakistani Christians. I, who lived far away, now I'm back in my country, to continue its mission to promote interfaith harmony, for the education and development of poor and marginalized communities. . . . Really being a Christian changes the life of a people! We Christians of Pakistan will not let the trials, difficulties, steal our hope, which is founded on the love of Jesus and the faith of the martyrs.

We will continue to witness to the Gospel of meekness, of dialogue, of love of enemies, of tenderness. This is our faith and this faith, which we want to live for and, if necessary, die for, as Shahbaz did.

Dear friends, I ask you all from the bottom of my heart, your neighborhood in the communion and prayer to Christians and to all the people of Pakistan: this gives us strength and frees us from fear. May God bring peace to our country and protect all people who are subject to violence and discrimination because of their faith. Do not forget us!

Two Sad Codas

As time wore on after Bhatti's death, there were developments that no doubt would have pained him, but that were perhaps inevitable given the climate in Pakistan and the fractured nature of a society in which sectarianism is often a way of life.

One such coda was the decision to eliminate the position he held in the federal government, minister for minorities affairs, in a cabinet reshuffle just four months after his death. Prior to 2004 there was a mid-level position for minority affairs within Pakistan's Ministry of Minorities, Culture, Sports, Tourism, and Youth Affairs, which was split off into a separate minister for minorities under President Pervez Musharraf. Upon the election of President Asif Ali Zadari from the leftist People's Party in 2008, the position was rechristened Minister for Minorities Affairs, given a significant increase in budget, and Bhatti was tapped to fill it.

In July 2011 it was announced that the position was being transformed into Minister for National Harmony, and that it would be occupied by Paul Bhatti, Shahbaz's oldest brother, in a clear sign of continuity. Paul Bhatti was also given the title Special Advisor to Prime Minister Yousuf Raza Gilani. He held that position until May 2013, when the People's Party was defeated in parliamentary elections. In June 2013 the new government under the conservative Pakistan Muslim League announced that the Ministry of National Harmony was being merged with the Ministry for Religious Affairs, effectively eliminating it as a cabinet-level position.

While a spokesperson for the new government insisted that the decision to fold the role into a larger ministry did not signal any retreat from concern for minority rights, but in fact would ensure that concern was at the center of the government's priorities rather than being marginalized in a small department, it might well depress Bhatti to know that once again there's no figure in Pakistan's cabinet whose main priority is the country's minority communities.

The other twist that might distress Bhatti was a splintering of the organization he founded, the All-Pakistan Minorities Alliance. In August 2013 one of the original members of the alliance, Tahir Naveed Chaudhry, announced that he was forming a rival group called the Pakistan Minorities Alliance: Voice of Minorities, because, as he put it, "after the martyrdom of Shahbaz Bhatti in 2011, the APMA could not deliver what was expected from it, so the true followers have decided to launch their own movement."

Chaudhry had been part of the 2002 All-Pakistan Minorities Convention in Islamabad that led to the founding of Bhatti's alliance, and later, in 2008, Bhatti nominated him as a candidate to run for the provincial assembly in Punjab, a race that Chaudhry won. He called himself the "backbone" of the APMA and "the most compatible and trustworthy companion of Shahbaz Bhatti," whom Chaudhry refers to as the "great leader."

Over time Chaudhry chafed under the new direction of the APMA led by Paul Bhatti, in part out of frustration that Paul Bhatti seemed excessively beholden to the Zadari government and the People's Party, which some Christians had come to regard as untrustworthy. Most observers, however, say it's not entirely clear whether the differences were over policy or were simply personality clashes.

Meanwhile Paul Bhatti continues on as the leader of the All-Pakistan Minorities Alliance, despite splitting his time between Pakistan and Italy. He announced in January 2016 during a Rome conference on anti-Christian persecution that he and the alliance founded by his brother would continue to press for abolition of Pakistan's blasphemy law.

Both leaders of the rival groups left behind by Shahbaz Bhatti, and countless others, have referred to Bhatti as a hero, a martyr, a champion of human rights, a leader, and a role model. For Catholics, however, confronted with the reality of someone who died vowing to give his life for Jesus Christ, one key question is whether another term may someday be added to that litany of titles, one with deep spiritual and ecclesiastic significance: Saint.

CHAPTER SIX

Sainthood

As fate would have it, the nine Catholic bishops of Pakistan were already scheduled to meet in March 2011, in Multan in Punjab, just eighteen days after Shahbaz Bhatti was shot to death on March 2 outside his Islamabad home. Inevitably the reality of the brutal assassination of the country's lone cabinet-level official, who was a Christian and also a Catholic, dominated their discussions.

While the bishops were understandably preoccupied with the need to press the Pakistani government for a serious investigation of Bhatti's murder and to ensure that the Christians of the country wouldn't feel abandoned after the loss of the figure many considered their primary champion and defender, they also had to consider how to process Bhatti's assassination from an internal, ecclesiastical point of view. It didn't take long for them to reach consensus. By a unanimous vote, they decided to petition Pope Benedict XVI to recognize Bhatti as a "martyr and patron of religious freedom" and that he be enrolled "in the martyrology of the universal church," effectively asking the pontiff to recognize Bhatti as a saint.

Benedict XVI didn't act on that request, and as a result the Pakistani bishops were compelled to wait out the normal five-year delay established in Catholic law for the formal opening of a sainthood process, which is understood as a sort of cooling-off period to ensure that the drive to see someone canonized isn't simply based on a fit of enthusiasm that might fade over time, but rather a genuine and enduring conviction that the person is a worthy candidate for a halo.

Obviously Bhatti passed that test for the bishops, because on March 2, 2016, five years to the day from Bhatti's death, the Diocese of Islamabad-Rawalpindi formally declared his sainthood cause open and said that officials would begin collecting the necessary testimony to compile the report to be submitted to the Vatican's Congregation for the Causes of Saints, called a *positio*, in order to evaluate whether Bhatti should be recognized as having lived a life of "heroic virtue." As a candidate, Bhatti can now be referred to by the title "Servant of God."

"He spoke with faith and demonstrated courage. Thanks to him the voice of Pakistan's Christians was heard. He paved the way for us. He was a good Catholic and gave his life for his mission," Archbishop Joseph Coutts of Karachi said at a March 2 ceremony marking the anniversary of Bhatti's death and the opening of his sainthood case. Ironically, the day happened to coincide with the funeral for Mumtaz Qadri, the bodyguard for Salmaan Taseer, the governor of Punjab and Bhatti's ally, who had assassinated Taseer while invoking the Qur'an. Qadri had been convicted by an antiterrorism court and sentenced to death, and was hanged on February 29. His funeral was held on March 2.

Over the centuries the Catholic Church has established painstaking standards to establish who qualifies as a saint and who doesn't, some of which are moral in nature and some spiritual. Moreover, it's also well-known that politics and other considerations can often speed or slow down a given sainthood cause, and it's never wise to be overly dogmatic about how any given cause will turn out. For many Pakistani Catholics, however, convinced that Bhatti is their patron in death just as he so often was in life, it's not a question of if but when.

Saint

In Catholic understanding, saints are not pure spirits but rather flesh and blood human beings who lived lives of great holiness and as a result enter directly into communion with God after death, meaning they're in heaven. Saints are believed to be powerful intercessors, who can carry prayers to God and ask for special favors and interventions. Catholics are encouraged to pray with the saints and to model their lives on their example. Despite the general emphasis in Catholicism on precision, there's actually no exact head count for the total number of recognized saints. The conventional estimate is that the church has recognized some 10,000 saints explicitly over the centuries, but Catholic belief also holds that there are countless additional saints in heaven whose holy lives were visible to God but were never recognized in a formal ecclesiastical process.

Generally speaking, saints acquire their reputation for holiness in at least one of three basic ways and sometimes through a combination of all three.

- giving their lives for the faith, a sacrifice that makes them a martyr;
- making life choices that exemplify extraordinary Christian virtue and fidelity to the Gospel (Mother Teresa would probably be the best modern example); and/or

- having supernatural gifts and wonder-working abilities. For instance, the famous Italian saint Padre Pio, formally known as St. Pio of Pietrelcina, who was believed to bear on his body the stigmata, meaning the five wounds of Christ.

Though Catholicism has a complicated procedure for reaching these judgments, technically speaking, Catholic theology holds that the church does not make saints, God does. All the church does is recognize what God has already accomplished in the life of a particular individual or group of believers. The tradition of identifying given individuals as saints dates back to the first century, and for a long stretch there wasn't any formal process. Saints were simply identified through popular acclamation and tradition. That was arguably a more democratic way to do things, but the lack of official quality control also meant that legend and historically dubious claims sometimes went unchecked. For instance, in 1969 the Vatican was forced to concede that there's little historical evidence for the existence of St. Christopher, formerly the popular patron saint of travelers whose feast day was dropped from the church's calendar.

The official review begins at the local level, with a bishop launching an inquiry into the life of the proposed saint to certify his or her personal virtue and doctrinal orthodoxy. Once that's complete the case is forwarded to the Vatican's Congregation for the Causes of Saints, where a panel of theologians looks over the material and makes a recommendation. The case then goes to the body of cardinals and other bishops who make up the congregation, and if the vote is favorable, it goes to the pope, who can decide to sign what's known as a "decree of heroic virtue" and declare the candidate "venerable."

The next step is known as beatification, and it generally requires proof of a miracle (except in the case of martyrs—more on that in a moment). Since a saint is supposed to be someone who's already in heaven, a miracle is considered proof that the person is indeed with God and capable of interceding on someone else's behalf, sort of God's seal of approval on the candidate. The miracle must occur after the person's death and in response to a specific request. In the vast majority of cases, the miracles in sainthood causes are healings from physical illness. These purported miracles are reviewed by a Vatican team of doctors and scientists who must certify that a healing is complete (just feeling better isn't enough), spontaneous, lasting, and without medical explanation. After beatification a candidate is referred to as "blessed," and that person's feast day can be celebrated by regions or groups of people for whom the person holds special importance.

The final step, canonization, requires proof of another miracle. When a new saint is canonized, his or her feast day is then opened up for the entire universal church. The act of canonization is considered to be infallible and irrevocable, so the church generally tries to be careful before it formally bestows the halo on someone. As of this writing, Bhatti is at the very beginning of the process, and it will depend on a variety of factors whether, and how quickly, his candidacy may move forward.

Church officials stress two additional points about the sainthood process. First, canonization is not a declaration that candidates never made a mistake. Instead, it's a finding that despite whatever failures or errors in judgment candidates committed during their earthly lives, their motives reflected personal integrity and commendable aims. Second, this is why the miracle requirement exists. If a legitimate miracle can be documented as attributable to a given candidate, it's proof of one's saintly status, regardless of whatever historical question marks may still surround the person's legacy.

Martyr

The term *martyr* is derived from the Greek word μάρτυς, a noun that in turn comes from the verb μαρτυρέω, or *marturéō*, which means "to give witness" or "to testify." It was used by the fifth-century BC historian Herodotus, for instance, when he wanted to support an argument of his own with a citation of Homer, and he suggested that Homer could "give witness" to the point. In Christian parlance, a martyr is thus someone who gives witness of the faith through the supreme sacrifice of his or her own life.

Traditionally, the test in Catholicism for which deaths qualify as instances of martyrdom has been that the person must have been killed *in odium fidei*, a Latin phrase meaning "in hatred of the faith." The idea is that simply giving one's life for another, while always noble and potentially even saintly on other grounds, is not enough to count as martyrdom. Instead, it has to be a case of a Catholic who was making a stand on the basis of one's religious convictions, and who was killed by people or forces explicitly hostile to those convictions. Thus in ancient Rome, a Christian who was killed for refusing to sacrifice to pagan gods would be regarded as a martyr, but one who was killed for political defiance of the emperor might not be, even if that defiance was rooted in faith, because the motives for the execution weren't necessarily overtly based on religious considerations.

Many times, the dividing line between what is and isn't a death *in odium fidei* has proven difficult to establish. The case of Archbishop Oscar Romero in El Salvador is emblematic. Romero was a celebrated champion of the poor in his country, a figure who stood against a right-wing military regime, demanding an end to human rights abuses and state-sanctioned terror, at one point shortly before his death ordering National Guard members to "Stop the repression!" On March 24, 1980, he was shot dead through the heart while saying Mass in a hospital chapel in San Salvador, and although no one was prosecuted for the murder, most Salvadorans believe the killers were linked to circles around former army Major Roberto D'Aubuisson.

Romero was quickly hailed as a martyr by many people around the world, but his sainthood case languished for thirty-five years in the Vatican. The delay was in part because of divisions among the Latin American hierarchy over the prudence of declaring Romero a saint, but it was also due to doubts about whether his murder qualified as a death *in odium fidei*. After all, both the men who plotted Romero's death and those who actually pulled the trigger were likely baptized Roman Catholics who had no specific animus against the faith and instead wanted Romero dead because he was frustrating their political and military ambitions.

That debate was settled in early February 2015, when Pope Francis signed a decree officially recognizing Romero as a martyr who had been killed *in odium fidei*, which cleared the way for his beatification in San Salvador later in the year.

Even had Pope Francis not been willing to certify that Romero had been assassinated in hatred of the faith, that might not have closed the conversation about whether Romero could be regarded as a martyr due to an evolution in the use of the term under St. Pope John Paul II, who stretched the concept of martyrdom to include not only those killed in hatred of the faith but also those who died *in odium caritatis,* or "in hatred of charity." Some theologians today are increasingly willing to include those killed out of hatred for the virtues inspired by the faith, not only for the articles of the faith itself.

One classic example is St. Maximilian Kolbe, a Polish Franciscan priest who died under the Nazis in the Auschwitz concentration camp in 1941 after volunteering to take the place of a stranger. This was not a death *in odium fidei,* because Kolbe wasn't put to death on the basis of his religious convictions. Yet when Pope John Paul II canonized Kolbe in 1982, the formal act of declaring someone a saint, he termed the Polish priest a "martyr of charity." Another case in point is Fr. Pino Puglisi, a prominent parish priest in Palermo, Sicily, known for his anti-mafia preaching and initiatives, who was beatified in 2013. He was killed in 1993 in retaliation for the thunderous denunciation of the mafia delivered by St. John Paul II on his visit to Sicily that year. Puglisi was, to use another well-established term, a martyr who died *in odium virtuosi et veritatis,* meaning "hatred of virtue and truth."

That language goes back to the canonization of Maria Goretti by the Venerable Pius XII in the holy year of 1950. The young girl had resisted the sexual advances of her teenage neighbor in 1902, who stabbed her more than a dozen times, and she died after having forgiven him. Goretti was not killed for her Catholic faith, but for her insistence on living the virtues it required. She preferred death to sin, and Pius XII declared her a martyr and saint.

Bhatti's Case for Martyrdom

At first blush, it would seem there's a very strong argument that Bhatti meets even the classic test of a death *in odium fidei* to be considered a martyr, which would mean there's no requirement for a miracle for him to be beatified. Typically a miracle would still be required to proceed to canonization, unless Francis or another pope were to decide to act in equipollent fashion, meaning setting aside many of the formal requirements for sainthood. While historically that's usually been done for candidates from long ago for whom it would be difficult to collect the required evidence, Francis declared Pope John XXIII, who died in 1963, a saint in equipollent fashion.

Perhaps the single most persuasive piece of evidence that Bhatti qualifies under the *in odium fidei* test is that his killers actually left behind literature describing him as a "Christian infidel" and a "blasphemer," which makes the religious subtext of the assassination reasonably obvious. Of course they were radical Muslim extremists, a force well-known for its explicit hatred of Christianity. That's essentially the same logic for why Fr. Jacques Hamel of France, an eighty-six-year-old priest whose throat was slit while saying Mass by two men professing allegiance to the Islamic State in July 2016, was swiftly proclaimed a martyr by many, including Pope Francis who said, "He is a martyr, and martyrs are beatified."

There certainly is no question about Bhatti's own religious motives, as his numerous references to wanting to live and die for Jesus Christ attest. He was a practicing, pious Roman Catholic, publicly identified as such, and linked his human rights and political activism to convictions rooted in his faith.

On the other hand, there are also complicating factors that the evaluators in the church's sainthood process will likely consider before reaching judgment.

First, although Bhatti's killers no doubt scorned his Christian faith, that probably wasn't the exclusive and perhaps not even the primary reason they shot him to death on

March 2, 2011. Instead, it was the fact that he had spoken out in defense of Asia Bibi, calling for her to be pardoned, and because he was leading a campaign to revise or abolish Pakistan's blasphemy laws. Like-minded radicals shortly before had killed a fellow Muslim, Taseer, for precisely the same reasons, so clearly creed wasn't really the decisive factor. In other words, the triggering incident for Bhatti's assassination was a set of political and legal positions with which he was associated, and even if both issues have clear religious overtones, evaluators in the sainthood cause may decide that disputes over the proper legal order of the state, in themselves, don't cross the threshold of being an *in odium fidei* case. That might be a harder case to make in the wake of the Romero beatification, but as the experience of sainthood causes over the centuries illustrate, every situation is different.

Second, there's also a question about Bhatti that's sometimes whispered among Christian observers in Pakistan, though rarely spoken in a clear voice because no one wants to question his heroism and sacrifice: Did he want martyrdom too much?

Traditionally, Catholicism cherishes its martyrs but takes a dim view of people who seem to lust for martyrdom, based in part on the sense that such a desire may betray a certain pride, a hunger for glory, that's unbecoming in a saint. That's the thrust of the famous scene in T. S. Eliot's *Murder in the Cathedral*, in which a tempter tries to induce St. Thomas à Becket to drop his battle with the king on the grounds that he wants martyrdom for motives of pride: "The last temptation is the greatest treason . . . to do the right deed for the wrong reason."

Over the years, some charged Bhatti with being excessively provocative and inflammatory with his public comments, almost at times as if he were waving a red flag in front of a bull. Some also thought he was a little too eager to associate his own hardships with Christ on the cross, seeing a self-aggrandizing streak in some of his rhetoric. While a great deal of these reactions likely could be chalked up to either envy or simple questions of personality differences, investigators probably will want to explore whether Bhatti was deliberately reckless in putting himself in harm's way.

For instance, they will likely make an effort to establish the truth of whether Bhatti did or didn't decline security protection the morning of his death, and whether, as had been reported, he also declined additional security when it had been offered. Some critics of Bhatti at the time of his death suggested he had run risks recklessly, almost courted them, in order to style himself as a hero and to bring attention to his cause.

Even if Bhatti's case is not determined to be an instance of *in odium fidei*, however, the argument for it qualifying as a death *in odium caritatis* seems almost impossible to dispute. His core priorities pivoted on the ideas of freedom of conscience, the defense of human rights and dignity, and the promotion of marginalized minority groups. Over the course of his life he practiced not only political charity in defense of those ideals but practical forms of service motivated by them as well, such as the relief effort he led after the 2005 earthquake. There's no real question that his killers hated the particular way Bhatti practiced those virtues, not to mention his effectiveness in attracting others to apply them as well, and killed him because of it.

The argument for declaring Bhatti a martyr *in odium fidei* seems compelling but not necessarily a slam dunk, while contesting the claim that he was a martyr *in odium caritatis* seems more difficult.

Bhatti as a Saint

One does not have to be declared a martyr in order to become a Catholic saint. For instance, when Popes John XXIII and John Paul II were canonized together in 2014, neither man became a saint as a martyr, because both died of natural causes in the Vatican. Even if Bhatti for some reason is not determined to be a martyr, that does not close the conversation as to whether he's worthy of a halo.

In many ways, the case seems straightforward. Bhatti clearly lived a life of heroic service, dedicating himself first to service and advocacy on behalf of his fellow Christians and then broadening his scope of concern to include all minorities in Pakistan. He also put his faith into action, sometimes even risking his own life in order to perform concrete acts of service on behalf of people in need. His faith is beyond question, and his moral virtue is equally undisputable—he was a Catholic layman who voluntarily embraced celibacy in order to make his commitment to service total.

Moreover, his cause checks several of the boxes that observers have traditionally identified while explaining why some sainthood causes move forward in the Catholic Church while others tend to languish. Generally speaking, there are six items on that list.

- An organization that is behind the cause and fully committed to it, with both the resources and the political savvy to move the ball.
- The cause represents a "first," meaning a candidate whose sainthood would recognize either a specific geographical region or an underrepresented constituency.
- A political or cultural issue symbolized by the candidate that lends a perceived sense of urgency.

- A sitting pope who feels a personal investment in the cause.

- Overwhelming hierarchical support, both from the bishops of the candidate's region and in Rome.

- Overwhelming popular support, such as the widespread Catholic conviction that Mother Teresa was a living saint or the chants of Santo Subito! meaning "sainthood now," heard from the crowd at Pope John Paul II's funeral Mass in April 2005.

To begin with, Bhatti does not really have a powerful organization connected to his cause, as he was neither the founder of a religious order nor a lay movement, and the bishops of Pakistan, while capable and devoted churchmen, are not generally known for the depth of their influence in the Vatican.

On the other hand, there is an organization, one with tremendous cachet in the Pope Francis era, which is invested in Bhatti's cause: the Community of Sant'Egidio, which has more or less become this pontiff's "go-to" movement, and which takes tremendous pride in its friendship with Bhatti over the years. Archbishop Vincenzo Paglia, currently the head of the Vatican's Pontifical Academy for Life and a core member of Sant'Egidio, was the postulator, or official in charge, of the Romero cause, and Sant'Egidio could perhaps tap his expertise to help advance Bhatti's candidacy as well.

Bhatti also would represent a "first," in the sense that there are no other Pakistani saints, and, for that matter, no saints, no matter where they were born, whose life or career were unambiguously rooted in modern-day Pakistan. (There are plenty of Sufi saints with ties to Pakistan, but that's another story.) Especially under Pope Francis, whose passion for the peripheries is the stuff of legend and who enjoys shining a spotlight on often-neglected and ignored corners of the world, the opportunity to canonize the first contemporary Pakistani saint might be tempting.

Further, there are at least two political and cultural motifs Bhatti embodies, both of which might have a special appeal for Pope Francis.

First, Bhatti would be the patron saint of new Christian martyrs, concern for whom is a frequent theme for Francis. The pontiff likes to point out that there are more martyrs today than in the early centuries of the church, and since those martyrs come from all Christian confessions, Francis also is fond of suggesting that their shared suffering is creating an "ecumenism of blood."

On the Feast of St. Stephen in late December 2016, Francis extolled the new Christian martyrs, saying, "Even today the Church, to render witness to the light and the truth, is beset in various places by hard persecutions, up to the supreme test of martyrdom." He continued, "How many of our brothers and sisters in the faith suffer abuses and violence, and are hated because of Jesus! The hardships and dangers notwithstanding, they offer courageous witness by belonging to Christ, and they live the Gospel committing themselves in favor of the least, of the most overlooked, doing good to all without distinction. They testify to charity in truth."

Canonizing Shahbaz Bhatti would certainly put an exclamation point on that truth about contemporary Christianity. Further, should his feast day be set on March 2, the date he was killed, as happened with Romero whose feast is March 24, then in effect March could become the "Month of the New Martyrs" on the Catholic calendar.

Second, Bhatti also symbolizes a cause especially near and dear to the heart of several recent popes, including Francis, which is the lay role in the Catholic Church. Bhatti was not a priest, a deacon, or a brother, and certainly not a bishop or a pope, but rather a layman who lived his faith as a human rights activist, a politician, and a government official.

Under St. John Paul II, who beatified and canonized more saints than all previous popes combined, there was a push to identify more candidates who were laity and especially women, on the grounds that they were underrepresented constituencies among the ranks of the church's formally recognized saints. Pope Francis in particular could be expected to be receptive to the idea of a contemporary lay candidate, since clericalism is a personal bête noire and the empowerment of laity a priority of his papacy. When Francis traveled to South Korea in the summer of 2014 and learned that the faith was planted in Korea not by missionary priests but by lay scholars, he lit up and extolled that history as a precious legacy for the entire church—and that would provide another factor that often explains why a sainthood cause succeeds, which is a personal investment by the current pope.

In terms of hierarchical support, the bishops of Pakistan went on record in support of the cause five years ago, and certainly Bhatti's legacy among the Christians of Pakistan has not dimmed over time. It's less clear what the opinion of Bhatti is among the power brokers in Rome, but given the deep concern in the Vatican today about anti-Christian persecution, there's no *a priori* reason to believe that Bhatti's candidacy would trigger any reflexive resistance.

Potential Complications

Despite all the considerations that might move Bhatti's candidacy forward, there are also good reasons to suspect that there may be a degree of caution that his candidacy might not move forward quite as quickly as a face-value reading of the situation might suggest.

First, as previously noted, there have been suggestions over the years that Bhatti may have been excessively pugnacious, confrontational, prideful, or reckless. To the extent that those traits, if established, could count against a finding of martyrdom, they would likely also be factors in considerations of sainthood.

Second, Bhatti drew strong criticism from some of his fellow Christians in Pakistan over the years. Some of his former colleagues in the Christian Liberation Front felt he was far too close to the Bhutto dynasty and the People's Party, and that he essentially sold his soul for political opportunity. Some also charged that Bhatti was a one-man show and used his rhetoric about anti-Christian persecution and the plight of the country's minorities to create a cult of personality around himself and to propel himself upon the national and international stage. It is likely that some of those Christians will be given an opportunity to testify during the process of collecting evidence in the sainthood process, and depending on what they have to say and how convincing the evaluators may find it, their perspectives could influence the eventual outcome.

Third is the possibility there may be some personally compromising aspect of Bhatti's life that never emerged publicly but which will come to light during the investigation phase of the process. Based on what we do know, that seems an improbable development, but one never knows.

Fourth, and perhaps most consequentially, there are some Pakistani bishops today who are quietly saying that pressing Bhatti's canonization right now might be a mistake, because it could produce political blowback that would be harmful to the local church.

Bhatti, after all, wasn't just a minority rights advocate, he was a politician. Specifically, he was a member of the Pakistan People's Party associated with former Prime Minister Benazir Bhutto and now led by her son, Bilawal Bhutto Zardari. It is today the country's largest opposition force to Prime Minister Nawaz Sharif and his Pakistan Muslim League. Many observers in Pakistan believe Sharif and his party would take a dim view of the canonization of someone so clearly associated with his rivals, seeing it as a form of interference in domestic politics. Further, it would also likely be taken as inflammatory by militant Islamic groups, and keeping those forces under control is always a national preoccupation.

For precisely those reasons, some bishops and other influential Catholic leaders in Pakistan feel somewhat ambivalent about Bhatti's cause, worrying that it may have negative political fallout and ask themselves, "What's the rush?" From a theological point of view, of course, that's absolutely right. If Bhatti is a saint, he's already in heaven enjoying the company of God, and his status won't be affected in the least by whether or not the church issues a formal recognition of it.

In fact, some Pakistani bishops are suggesting that Bhatti may not even be the country's best candidate for sainthood right now. Instead, they point to Akash Bashir, a twenty-year-old Catholic from Youhanabad in Pakistan's Lahore region who gave his life in 2015 to try to stop a suicide bomber from attacking St. John Catholic Church of Lahore. Seventeen people were killed and dozens were wounded when two suicide bombers blew themselves up at two churches on March 15, 2015, in the biggest Christian settlement of Lahore. The death toll would undoubtedly have been much higher had Bashir not intercepted one of the bombers and stopped him from entering the church.

"We have started gathering information at the grassroots level, because the cause can begin anytime," Father Francis Gulzar, pastor at St. John's, told *Our Sunday Visitor*, and added that Archbishop Joseph Coutts, president of the Pakistani bishops' conference, is planning to petition the Holy See to allow the formal launch of a cause for beatification and canonization of Bashir. Posters of him are still pasted on the walls of churches and shops of Youhanabad, home to more than 10,000 Christian families, 70 percent of whom are Catholics.

Arguably, Bashir's death is an even more clear-cut case of a death *in odium fidei,* since it came amid an attack on a church. As a Pakistani, he too would be a "first," and he was also a lay Catholic. Moreover, there are no political complications in his case, since he was never involved in party politics and never held a governmental position.

From the point of view of eternity, of course, it really doesn't matter which Pakistani candidate for sainthood is the first across the finish line. For people who knew and admired Bhatti, however, they will no doubt hope that the sum total of his life and legacy quickly outweighs the possible blemishes on his record or the political complications his cause may create.

Conclusion

In the end, no matter what judgment the local bishops of Pakistan or officials in the Vatican may reach about Shahbaz Bhatti as a candidate for sainthood, there's no question that he belongs on any list of the most remarkable Catholic personalities of the last fifty years. His strong Catholic faith and unique personal drive propelled him into positions and situations that form a riveting Catholic saga.

The high points of that saga: Born into a devout Catholic family in 1968, from early on Bhatti was basically intoxicated by the faith. He became an altar boy and assisted priests in celebrating Mass, giving him a chance to move around with them to villages and see how Christians truly lived in a country where they were fewer than 2 percent of the population, with most of them consigned to illiteracy, poverty, and chronic second-class citizenship. Bhatti would later recall that when he was thirteen, he heard a Good Friday sermon about the sacrifice of Jesus on the cross and decided then and there he would dedicate his life to defending Christians and other minorities in the country.

In college he founded an organization for Christian students to help them stand up to the pressures of Islamic radicalism, which was then just gathering force across the

Muslim world and didn't look kindly on the presence of Christian students even in state-run universities.

Bhatti said he was grabbed and beaten, even tortured, on several occasions to try to compel him to renounce his activism, but he steadfastly refused. Later, Bhatti founded the group for which he became known, the All-Pakistan Minorities Alliance, which campaigned for the rights of Christians and other minority groups, such as Hindus, Ahmadis, and secularists.

In addition to political and legal advocacy, Bhatti's alliance also had a strong humanitarian emphasis. When a devastating 7.6 magnitude earthquake rocked Kashmir in October 2005, the group was on the front lines of the relief effort, digging bodies out of the rubble, donating blood, organizing tents and soup kitchens, and teaching children whose schools had been destroyed. All that gave Bhatti a national profile, and in November 2008 he was named Federal Minister for Minorities Affairs, making him the lone Christian in the Pakistani cabinet.

From that perch, Bhatti continued to press for reform, among other things emerging as the country's most forceful critic of so-called blasphemy laws used to criminalize a wide range of speech and behavior seen as un-Islamic. He took up the cause of Asia Bibi, an illiterate, Catholic farmhand and mother of five from a village in the Punjab who had been sentenced to death under the blasphemy law following a dispute with some village women over access to drinking water.

Bhatti knew full well his positions made him a marked man, even recording a video to be released in the event he was murdered in which he said, "I believe in Jesus Christ who has given his own life for us, and I am ready to die for a cause. I'm living for my community . . . and I will die to defend their rights."

He was eventually shot to death outside his home in a residential district of Islamabad on March 2, 2011, executed by members of the radical Muslim group Tehrik-i-Taliban, which left pamphlets behind describing Bhatti as a "Christian infidel" and "blasphemer."

Virtually every element of his life story is impressive, with obvious drawing power in terms of firing the imagination. And there are three aspects of his life and legacy that could also appeal to Christian minds, hearts, and souls in the early twenty-first century.

Brashness

Through the ages Catholics have struggled with one aspect of the life stories of saints: in addition to their deep holiness or spiritual power, many of them also seem almost impossibly, well, nice. They're forever ready to forgive wrongs, suffer hardships in silence, and make themselves the least among us and spurn the lures of worldly ambition and fame. Those are all highly admirable qualities, of course, but they sometimes seem almost alien to the experience of most ordinary people.

Bhatti, however, comes off differently. For one thing, he was nobody's idea of a milquetoast personality. He did anything but suffer wrongs in silence. Instead, he spoke out, forcefully and loudly, and he fought back—admittedly through politics and advocacy campaigns, not through violence, but there was a definite pugnaciousness about Bhatti, even perhaps at times a bit of a thin skin, that's recognizably human.

Bhatti was hardly one to shun the spotlight. On the contrary, he seemed to relish it, rarely saying no to interview requests or speaking engagements, and in general often making himself the center of attention. In his heart, of course, he saw that platform as an opportunity to advance the causes to which he'd given his life, especially minority rights and interfaith harmony. Nevertheless, a handful of critics during his lifetime charged he was egotistical and borderline narcissistic, almost addicted to celebrity and far too eager to celebrate his own accomplishments. Even if there's some small degree of truth to those complaints, arguably they don't make Bhatti any less saintly but, rather, more accessible to plenty of people who may struggle with the same temptations and flaws.

Many contemporary Christians probably can connect with the swagger Bhatti often projected, his steely resolve not to take insult and injury lying down. There's a mounting sense across the Christian world that many Christians have been too passive in the face of anti-Christian persecution, too consumed by a form of political correctness that dictates not rocking the boat, not risking giving offense. That was not the ethos of Shahbaz Bhatti, who never saw a fight he wasn't willing to take on, and who exuded a kind of non-violent muscularity that's inspiring for Christians who think now is the time to push back. Being meek and mild are time-honored Christian virtues, but there's also a role in Christian life for strength and grit. That was a large part of the appeal of St. John Paul II, for instance, and they are qualities Bhatti had in spades as well.

When Taseer and Bhatti were murdered around the same time, many observers noted the odd couple dynamic of their partnership. While both were completely committed to the idea of Pakistan as a secular, democratic state in which the rights of minorities are assured, in keeping with the vision of the country's founding father, Muhammad Ali Jinnah, in terms of personality types they were very different. Taseer was refined, wealthy, delicate, and a true gentleman. Bhatti, by way of contrast, lived simply, almost monastically, and sometimes came off as coarse, rough-and-tumble, and as a street brawler, almost daring anyone to knock the chip off his shoulder. Writing in the *New York Times* in March 2011, Jane Perlez described the two men as "one quiet, one brash."

Bhatti, in other words, is sort of a patron saint for the alpha male.

Though it may seem counterintuitive, especially in light of perceptions that the Catholic Church is often a boy's club, some writers actually have fretted that Christian spirituality is excessively feminine in tone and emphasis. David Murrow's *Why Men Hate Going to Church* (Thomas Nelson, 2004) and Leon J. Podles's *The Church Impotent: The Feminization of Christianity* (Spence, 1999) illustrate the point. Murrow is a Presbyterian and Podles a Catholic, but both have noticed something similar about their respective denominations.

Podles believes that Western Christianity has been feminizing itself for the better part of one thousand years, beginning with medieval imagery about the church as the "Bride of Christ," which he associates with St. Bernard of Clairvaux, and exhortations to "fall in love" with Jesus. While that kind of imagery has a powerful impact on women, Podles wrote, it's off-putting for men.

Murrow, a media and advertising specialist, basically agreed: "If our definition of a 'good Christian' is someone who's nurturing, tender, gentle, receptive and guilt-driven, it's going to be a lot easier to find women who will sign up," he wrote. Both men contend the spirituality gap is reflected in the fact that almost anywhere you go in the Christian world, you're likely to find more women in church than men.

As Podles put it succinctly, "Women go to church, men go to football games."

If it's true that Christianity needs more role models of how to be both saintly and tough, how to seek God without shrinking from a fight, then Shahbaz Bhatti is ideally cut out for the role. He was brash and bold, and while some might argue those qualities occasionally shaded off into recklessness or seeking confrontation for its own sake, in the main they are virtues rather than vices, and ones relatively few Christian heroes project in quite the same way.

The Right Kind of Interfaith Dialogue

In theory there is absolutely no conflict between mounting a strong defense of persecuted Christians and being deeply sensitive to the importance of good relations with other religions. In fact, there's an utterly convincing case to be made that the two are vitally related, because the persecution many Christians suffer is inflicted on them by followers of other faiths, whether it's Islam in the Middle East, Hinduism in India, or even Buddhism in Myanmar, and to combat it, Christian activists and leaders need allies within those religious communities.

In practice, however, these two aims—defending Christians and the rights of the church, and cultivating ties with other faiths—often seem to be at odds. Christians most invested in interreligious dialogue are often hesitant to stand up aggressively for Christian interests, fearing it will come off as either confessional or provocative, while Christians most passionate about defending the church sometimes look askance at ecumenical and interfaith dialogue, fearing it may end up as an excuse for going soft. Examples of that dichotomy abound, from experts in Christian-Muslim dialogue who object to demonizing Islam whenever someone speaks out about the atrocities inflicted on Christians by ISIS, to artisans of Catholic dialogue with the Russian Orthodox who shrink from being too confrontational about Russia's aggression in Ukraine and its hostility to the Greek Catholic Church for fear that it may fray ties with Moscow.

In that context the church could sorely use an exemplar of how the right answer is both/and rather than either/or, how dialogue can be both firm and friendly at the same time, and how defending Christians and reaching out to other faiths actually is a package deal. That, in a nutshell, is a core part of the Shahbaz Bhatti legacy.

As we have seen, no one in recent memory was more dogged, more relentless, in defending Christians at risk than Bhatti. As he put it, "I always consider that my human body is wounded, but these wounds are not physical, they are the worries, the griefs, the sorrows, and pain of the persecuted Christians of Pakistan, of the needy and oppressed Christians." Far from feeling that discretion was the better part of valor, Bhatti had a zero-tolerance approach to discrimination against Christians—from small slights to massive forms of second-class citizenship, Bhatti took it all on with verve, and for thirty years few voices in the world thundered more loudly about anti-Christian persecution than his.

At the same time, Bhatti was also seen within Pakistan and around the world as a hero of interfaith dialogue. Few Christians in the country had a wider network of relationships with Muslims, Hindus, Sikhs, Ahmadis, and other religious groups, and he had enormous street credibility within those communities for his fervent advocacy of their rights. Peter Bhatti, one of Shahbaz's brothers, recalled after his brother's death that he "loved the idea of interfaith harmony and tolerance," and during his term as the minister of minorities, promoting seminars, workshops, and training courses on interfaith dialogue was among Bhatti's core priorities. He made a point of meeting global Christian leaders to urge greater support for interfaith efforts, such as then-Archbishop of Canterbury Rowan Williams and French Cardinal Jean-Louis Tauran, head of the Vatican's Pontifical Council for Interreligious Dialogue. One of his main attractions to the Community of Sant'Egidio was the annual interfaith summit they sponsored that had been inspired by St. John Paul II's historic 1986 interreligious gathering in Assisi. He also received an honorary doctorate from the University of South Korea for his leadership in interfaith dialogue.

However, Bhatti's vision of dialogue had a price of admission—accepting the principle of religious freedom as a nonnegotiable value. He was never shy about speaking out when he felt elements of a particular religious community were backsliding on that principle or openly rejecting it, as was the case with his ferocious campaign against Pakistan's blasphemy laws. Bhatti had a clear-eyed vision that the real clash in the early twenty-first century isn't one religion versus another, but rather fanatics and extremists of all faiths against believers in pluralism and tolerance.

In that sense Bhatti was a pioneer in the kind of interfaith dialogue the contemporary era desperately needs, and his example has lost none of its relevance after his death.

Symbol of Contemporary Christianity

If someone were to stage a contest to see who could come up with the best one-sentence description of Christian history in the twentieth century, the winning entry would probably be some version of the following: the center of gravity shifted from north to south.

According to the World Christian Database, by the year 2025 there will be about 2.6 billion Christians on earth (compared to 2 billion today), of whom 633 million will live in Africa, 640 million in Latin America, and 460 million in Asia. Europe, with 555 million, will have slipped to third place, with Asia hard on its heels. To take Bhatti's continent of Asia as an example, Christianity went from 2.3 percent of the population in 1900 to almost 9 percent today. Sometime soon, if it hasn't happened already, there will be more Christians in Asia than Buddhists—a mind-bending reversal of normal impressions about the continent's preferred religion.

This trajectory is crystal clear in Catholicism. In 1900 at the dawn of the twentieth century, there were roughly 266.5 million Catholics in the world, according to *Global Catholicism: Portrait of a World Church*, of whom more than 200 million were in Europe and North America, and just 66 million scattered across the entire rest of the planet. In 2000 by way of contrast, there were slightly under 1.1 billion Roman Catholics in the world, of whom just 350 million were Europeans and North Americans. The overwhelming majority, a staggering 720 million people, lived in Latin America, Africa, and Asia. Almost half the Catholic total, more than 400 million people, lived in Latin America alone.

Projecting forward slightly, by the year 2025 only one Catholic in five in the world will be a non-Hispanic Caucasian. This is the most rapid, and most sweeping, demographic transformation of Roman Catholicism in its two-thousand-year history.

This truth about contemporary Christianity, however, is often ignored or forgotten in much public conversation. Say "anti-Christian persecution" to many Americans, and they think you're talking about the Affordable Care Act contraception mandates or the ability of county clerks to dissent from gay marriage laws, not a low-caste nun in India being raped and savagely beaten by Hindu radicals. When Pope Francis extols the virtues of the poor, Westerners often flash on (terribly exaggerated) images of Vatican wealth, not the vast majority of the world's Christian population, especially in the global south, that lives in chronic poverty.

In that sense the world could use a high-profile figure who brings home the reality of Christian life in the early twenty-first century, and once again no one is better cut out for the part than Shahbaz Bhatti.

Aside from the obvious fact that Bhatti himself is non-Western, his life story pivots on the discovery of how most Christians today actually live. As chapter one outlines, he was born in a traditionally Catholic village in Punjab, into a family that certainly wasn't wealthy but also wasn't poor, especially by local standards. As he became a committed altar boy and started traveling with priests to neighboring villages and met the Christian communities in those places, he was stunned by the chronic poverty, the marginalization, and the oppression those Christians faced on a daily basis. The experience changed his life, propelling him on a course of striving to serve those Christians and eventually other minorities who struggled with similar hardships, which ultimately led to a martyr's death.

To learn about Shahbaz Bhatti is to learn what Christian experience is really like in our time.

To be sure, these three aspects of the Shahbaz Bhatti story—his brashness, his model of interfaith dialogue, and the way he symbolizes contemporary Christianity—are not the heart of his appeal. Instead, what makes him so compelling is the unvarnished fact of a man who lived and died for Jesus Christ and for the oppressed and needy in whom he saw Christ's face. Beyond that, his drawing power is also the way he embodies the whole story of anti-Christian persecution, the great Christian drama and human rights scourge of our time. Yet these three points do help explain why, should Bhatti one day be canonized, he would be such a powerful symbol, a patron of several urgent and crucially important causes.

They also help explain why, regardless of what happens with his sainthood cause, the story of Shahbaz Bhatti is worth telling—always and everywhere, over and over again, until it's part of the common patrimony of Christianity and of all humanity.

Index

Abdullah, Umer, 83
Ahmad, Iftikhar, 91
Ahmadis, 41, 45, 47, 56, 117, 122
Ahmadiyya, 44
All-Pakistan Minorities Alliance (APMA), 2, 24, 39, 40–57, 84, 87, 96–97, 117
All-Pakistan Minorities Convention, 39, 41, 96
Al-Qaeda, 59, 79, 86
Anthony, Rufin (bishop), 14, 19–20, 75, 87, 91
assassination of Bhatti, 11, 78–84, 98, 106, 107; foreshadowing of, 84–87; reaction to, 87–95

Barwa, John (archbishop), 7
Barwa, Sr. Meena Lalita, 7
Bashir, Akash, 114–15
beatification. *See* sainthood
Benedict XVI (pope), 3, 65, 66, 70, 71, 75–76, 88–89, 98–99
Bhatti family, 2, 3, 15–17, 18–19, 49–50, 78, 80, 82, 85, 87, 125. *See also* Bhatti, Paul

Bhatti, Jacob, 15–16, 78
Bhatti, Jacqueline, 3
Bhatti, Mariam, 80
Bhatti, Paul, 11, 16, 18–19, 83, 92–95, 95–96, 97
Bhatti, Peter, 16, 122
Bhatti, Sikander, 17, 83, 87
Bhutto, Benazir, 50–51, 59–60, 61, 114
Bhutto, Zufikar, 59
Bibi, Asia, 3, 30–32, 70–77, 107, 117
Bible, 11, 16, 49, 94
blasphemy laws, 14, 29, 30–33, 35, 36, 38, 45, 46, 52, 70–77; Bhatti working toward abolition of, 2–3, 21, 22, 23, 46, 52, 61–62, 68–70, 71–74, 76–77, 79, 80, 84, 85, 86, 89, 91, 97, 107, 117, 123
Boko Haram, 7
Buddhism, 121, 124

Candelin, Johan, 86
canonization. *See* sainthood
Capuchin missionaries, 13, 14, 26, 27–28

Caritas, 29, 55
caste. *See* classes, social
Catholic Church in Pakistan, 3, 13–14, 15, 16, 25–28, 29, 98–99, 114–115
Chaudhry, Cecil, 22–23, 92
Chaudhry, Tahir Naveed, 96–97
Chellen, Fr. Thomas, 7
Christian Liberation Front, 19, 23, 42, 51, 91, 113
Christianity, 5, 17–18, 25–26, 31–32, 111, 120–21, 123–26
Christians. *See* religious persecution: of Christians
church. *See* Catholic Church in Pakistan; Vatican
classes, social, 9, 16–17, 17–18, 26, 27–28, 33, 68, 125
Clinton, Hillary, 89–90
Cordiero, Joseph (cardinal), 29
Coutts, Joseph (archbishop), 87, 99, 115

Da Vinci Code, The, 52
death penalty abolition, 67
democracy, 11, 23, 41, 51, 62, 69, 91, 119
Dike, Chioma, 7
discrimination. *See* blasphemy laws; religious persecution; women, discrimination/abuse of

Exit Control List, 50
extremism, 2, 32, 41, 42, 49–50, 56, 60, 69, 72, 74, 76, 85, 91, 106, 123

family of Bhatti. *See* Bhatti family *and specific names following*
Felix, Fr., 13
Francis (pope), 37, 38, 93, 104, 106, 110–11, 112, 125

Gilani, Yousuf Raza, 88, 96
Gill, Simon Jacob, 14, 51
Goretti, Maria, 105

Hamel, Fr. Jacques, 106
Hinduism, 25, 27, 44, 63, 121. *See also* Hindus
Hindus, 4, 11, 25, 27, 28, 38, 41, 44, 45, 56, 63, 94, 117, 122. *See also* Hinduism
humanitarian relief efforts, 8–9, 16, 47, 48, 52–57, 117

illiteracy, 3, 9, 18, 30, 71, 116, 117
in odium caritatis, 105, 108
in odium fidei, 103–7, 108, 115
interfaith dialogue, 62, 65, 67, 69, 70, 75, 86, 90, 94, 119, 121–23, 125
International Islamic University, Islamabad, 67–68
ISIS, 8, 106, 122
Islam, 26, 28, 44, 45, 58, 121, 122. *See also* Muslims

Jesuits, 26
Jews, 9, 79
Jinnah, Muhammad Ali, 28, 41, 63, 92, 119

John Paul II, St., 1, 21, 40–41, 104, 105, 109, 110, 112, 119, 123
John XXIII, St., 29, 106, 109
Joseph, John (bishop), 14–15
Jundallah, 37

Kenny, Jason, 81, 85
Khan, Maulana Mehfooz, 90
Khushpur, Pakistan, 13–14, 19, 24, 51, 87, 91, 93
Kolbe, St. Maximilian, 105

Mandela, Nelson, 1
martyrdom, 100, 102, 103–5, 109, 111; of Bhatti, 4, 10–11, 98, 105–8, 111, 113
Masih, Abas, 82
Masih, Amarish, 36
Masih, Ayub, 14–15
Masih, Pervaiz, 67–68
Masih, Rimsha, 33
Minister for Minorities Affairs, 2, 58, 61–77, 94, 95, 117
Minister for National Harmony, 95–96
minorities. *See* Ahmadis; All-Pakistan Minorities Alliance (APMA); blasphemy laws; Hindus; Minister for Minorities Affairs; religious persecution; Sikhs
miracles, 102–3, 106
Mother Teresa, 29, 100, 110
Musharraf, Pervez (president), 42, 50, 51, 59, 95

Muslims, 5, 11, 25, 27, 29, 44–45, 54, 56, 90, 94, 122. *See also* Islam

Obama, Barack (president), 89
Ooberfuse, 4

Paglia, Vincenzo (archbishop), 110
Pakistan Christian Congress, 66
Pakistan Muslim League, 51, 66, 96, 114
Pakistan People's Party, 33, 51, 59–60, 61, 62, 66, 69, 73, 76, 95, 96, 97, 113, 114
Paul VI (pope), 29
persecution. *See* religious persecution
Pfau, Sr. Ruth, 29
Puglisi, Fr. Pino, 105

Qadri, Malik Mumtaz Hussain, 74, 75, 82, 99
Qur'an, 32, 33, 34, 36, 65, 99

Rehman, Sherry, 33, 73, 76, 80
religious persecution, 45; Bhatti working against, 10–11, 17–18, 18–21, 23–24, 40–44, 47–48, 57, 61, 86–87, 93; of Christians, 4–10, 14–15, 26, 31–32, 34–39, 43, 65, 79, 82, 88, 119, 121–22, 124–26. *See also* Bibi, Asia; blasphemy laws
Romero, Oscar (archbishop), 85, 104, 107, 110, 111

sainthood, 99–103, 104, 105, 109–10, 111–12, 114–15; Bhatti's, 3, 12, 48, 98–100, 102, 105–15; "secular," 1, 11
Saldhana, Lawrence (archbishop), 76, 91–92
Sant'Egidio, 67, 92, 93, 94, 110, 123
secularism, 28, 46, 59, 60, 69, 76, 77, 91, 92, 117, 119
Servant of God, 4, 99
Shah, Syed Najeeb Ali, 91
Shakir, Inayat Ali, 90
sharia laws, 46, 60, 86, 91
Sikhism, 27
Sikhs, 4, 11, 54, 56, 62, 63, 94, 122
Sindhu, Khalil Tahir, 20–21
sweepers, 17–18, 33

Taliban, 16, 37, 42, 63, 68, 75, 85, 86. *See also* Tehrik-i-Taliban
Taseer, Salmaan, 3, 11, 72, 74–75, 80, 82, 84, 85, 91, 99, 107, 119–20
Tauran, Jean-Louis (cardinal), 71, 123
Tehrik-i-Taliban, 3, 80, 79, 83, 118
terrorism, 3, 5, 7, 24, 34–35, 37, 42, 44, 47, 62, 65, 67–68, 83, 84, 99, 114. *See also* Al-Qaeda; Boko Haram; ISIS; Jundallah; Taliban; Tehrik-i-Taliban

United States, 5, 8, 9, 33, 37, 42, 80, 89–90
University of the Punjab, Lahore, 19–21
University, International Islamic, Islamabad, 67–68

Vacca Ramirez, Misael (bishop), 7–8
Vatican, 27, 52, 71, 75, 88, 123, 125. *See also* sainthood
Vatican II, 14, 15

Wilam, Regina Elsa, 14
Williams, Rowan (archbishop), 123
women, discrimination/abuse of, 46–47, 61
Women's Protection Bill, 46

Zardari, Asif Ali (president), 60, 62, 65, 66, 67, 70, 71, 73, 80
Zardari, Bilawal Bhutto, 60, 114
Zia-ul-Haq, Muhammad (president), 20, 29, 46, 59
Zulfiqar, Chaudhry, 83

www.ingramcontent.com/pod-product-compliance
Lightning Source LLC
Chambersburg PA
CBHW070527010526
44110CB00050B/2192